D0559285

The Christian Humanism
of Flannery O'Connor

BW
9.95
9-26-78

The Christian Humanism
of Flannery O'Connor

by *David Eggenschwiler*
UNIVERSITY OF SOUTHERN CALIFORNIA

Wayne State University Press, Detroit, 1972

Copyright © 1972 by Wayne State University Press,

Detroit, Michigan 48202. All rights are reserved.

No part of this book may be reproduced without formal permission.

Published simultaneously in Canada

by The Copp Clark Publishing Company

517 Wellington Street, West, Toronto 2B, Canada.

Library of Congress Cataloging in Publication Data
Eggenschwiler, David, 1936–
    The Christian humanism of Flannery O'Connor.
    Bibliography: p.
        1. O'Connor, Flannery. 2. Humanism, Religious.
I. Title.
PS3565.C57Z665   211'.6   79-179560
ISBN 0-8143-1463-5

    The author gratefully acknowledges permission to quote from the following
works:
    Wise Blood, copyright © 1949, 1952, 1962 by Flannery O'Connor; The
Violent Bear It Away, copyright © 1955, 1960 by Flannery O'Connor; Every-
thing That Rises Must Converge, copyright © 1956, 1957, 1958, 1960, 1961,
1962, 1964, 1965 by the Estate of Mary Flannery O'Connor; Mystery and
Manners, selected and edited by Sally and Robert Fitzgerald, copyright ©
1957, 1961, 1963, 1964, 1966, 1967, 1969 by the Estate of Mary Flannery
O'Connor, copyright © by Flannery O'Connor, copyright © 1961 by Farrar,
Straus & Cudahy, Inc. Reprinted by permission of Farrar, Straus & Giroux,
Inc.
    A Good Man Is Hard to Find, copyright © 1955 by Flannery O'Connor.
Reprinted by permission of Harcourt Brace Jovanovich, Inc.

Contents

Preface

$\mathcal{I}n$ focusing this study on a single thesis, that Flannery O'Connor consistently wrote from the point of view of a Christian humanist, I have slighted important aspects of her fiction, most obviously her humor, regionalism, and use of the grotesque.[1] Since there are already several general surveys of her work, I have not tried to be inclusive or introductory. Assuming that readers need no longer feel the perplexities shown by some of Miss O'Connor's early reviewers, I have bypassed points of major critical agreement to concentrate on objections that have not been adequately met, and I have tried to show that the Christian humanism Miss O'Connor held in common with many Catholic and Protestant theologians provides the best grounds for the defense.

First, her humanism should largely disprove the charges that her view of life was religiously, psychologically, and socially provincial, that, apart from her strictly religious allegory, her main concerns were peripheral and exotic. By showing her similarities with some of the most influential modern theologians, psychologists, and sociologists, I hope to demonstrate that her work relates closely to modern intellectual traditions

Preface

and that she explores problems that have preoccupied men who are central to modern humanism. Beyond this apologetic aim, the use of various disciplines also helps to bring out the thematic richness of individual works by showing that a resonant religious theme will involve many human concerns to achieve its full expression. Finally, this approach should also help to uncover some of the structural principles behind her work, to show that a belief in the coherence of the world can help to create a complexly coherent literature. More specifically, it can answer some of the charges that her works contain unprepared climaxes, confused authorial attitudes, and overly manipulated characters.

I want to thank the Leo S. Bing Fund and the University of Southern California for financial grants throughout my preparation of this study; Kittsu Barks for first encouraging me to begin this work; and the editors of *Renascence* for permitting me to adapt portions of my article, "Flannery O'Connor's True and False Prophets," which was published in their Spring 1969 issue. Above all, I want to thank my wife, Jean, for her help, criticism, and understanding.

D.E.

1. Introduction:

The Whole Horse

This modern mind sees only half of the horse—that half which may become a dynamo, or an automobile, or any other horse-powered machine. If this mind had much respect for the full-dimensioned, grass-eating horse, it would never have invented the engine which represents only half of him. The religious mind, on the other hand, has this respect; it wants the whole horse, and it will be satisfied with nothing less.

Allen Tate [1]

In the forty-one years since Allen Tate wrote his essay on Southern religion for the Agrarian manifesto, *I'll Take My Stand,* some of the most influential writers on religion and the social sciences have joined in the search for the whole horse. This search is not unique to the present, nor are many of the current attempts to explain the dismemberment of the horse. Since William Blake and his contemporaries insisted that man had hidden in the cave of his skull, allowing only manageable fragments of reality to enter through the chinks of the cavern, man's reduction of existence has been a central theme of writers in various fields—Kierkegaard, Nietzsche, Yeats, Bergson, Whitehead, Lawrence. Yet the past few decades have shown a wider concern with the problem than ever before. In fact, some of the recent popular movements, such as the use of mind-expanding drugs, the creation of rural communes, the influence of Eastern religions, suggest a growing discontent with the half-horse of positivism and utility. So it is hardly surprising that many important social critics have reacted against specialization of knowledge and have tried to understand social problems in the terms of religion, psychology, and philosophy.

9

Many theologians also have realized that religion must not be separated from other concerns; as Allen Tate claimed in the work cited above, the horse is not "just an infinite object" any more than it is just an engine (p. 158). Trying to avoid surrendering the world either to the devil or to science, these theologians and religious philosophers have used disciplines which, in themselves, have often been antagonistic to religion. For example, Reinhold Niebuhr uses Marxist insights into the irrationality and hypocrisy of economic behavior. M. C. D'Arcy and Romano Guardini use Freudian and Jungian psychology in their studies of Christian love. And existentialism has had an enormous influence on both Protestant and Catholic commentators. Of course, these secular disciplines must undergo a sea-change for the ends of a God they were not intended to serve; otherwise, religion would fail to see the whole horse and would be left only with a horse-powered machine called "social ethics" or "spiritual dynamics," another useful engine with a touch of sanctity. The best of the eclectic theologians have emphasized the incomplete views of the disciplines they have incorporated: Reinhold Niebuhr attacks Marx's assumption that man is basically an economic animal; D'Arcy denies Freud's pessimism by denying his biological determinism; Tillich claims that existentialism gives much to theology by analyzing the human situation but that the answers to its questions must come from outside the situation itself. They are quite aware that these disciplines have been used idolatrously to cut existence down to manageable size, to stuff it completely within the knowable and systematic. But they also know that one can be so afraid of idolatry that one retreats to another false extreme, refusing to admit the religious value of natural understanding. As Jacques Maritain has stated, philosophy (as opposed to theology) aspires to a better knowledge than its own "not in so far as it knows its proper object *badly*, but in so far as it knows it *well*." [2] Maritain himself advocates a Thomistic synthesis in which various disciplines serve their own ends within a hierarchy, and he regrets that the natural sciences and metaphysics have not only been separated, which is proper, but isolated, which might be literally disastrous.

Assuming that such intellectually synthetic approaches are not only valuable but necessary at the present time, I have appropriated whatever I have found pertinent and enlightening in various disciplines for use in studying Flannery O'Connor. Such an approach seems especially helpful when applied to this author, who had a great respect for the whole horse, who saw life from many perspectives, but who also believed that what she saw was a whole that demanded complex and integrated responses from the writer. Throughout her essays and lectures Miss O'Connor repeatedly claimed that the novelist writes "with the whole personality" and that "great fiction involves the whole range of human judgment." [3] She insisted that the ultimate concerns of her art transcended the natural but that her art was primarily of the concrete world in which the transcendent was manifested. To paraphrase Maritain, I believe that she sought a more than worldly knowledge, not by knowing the world badly but by knowing it well, by seeing more of it than we usually permit ourselves to see. If such vision is characteristic of the prophet, the seer, it is also characteristic of the true humanist, what Maritain calls the "theocentric humanist," who considers man in his full complexity without being compelled to elevate or debase him by closing one eye. Such a humanist considers man in his finite and infinite extensions, as a creature of religious, psychological, and social depths. And, since he considers existence to be a whole, he finds these dimensions necessarily related.[4]

In Miss O'Connor's lectures on her writing two subjects occur more than any other, and they are complementary concerns of the Christian humanist. First, she insisted that the fiction writer needs to have "anagogical vision," the ability "to see different levels of reality in one image or one situation," and she wrote that "the Catholic sacramental view of life is one that sustains and supports at every turn the vision that the storyteller must have if he is going to write fiction of any depth" (*Mystery and Manners*, pp. 72, 152). Even a casual reader must become aware of these "added dimensions" in her work. One can hardly ignore the overt religious metaphors that suggest sacramental vision (a sun that looks like a blood-drenched host, a peacock that suggests the transfiguration), or the authorial comments that grace has been given to a character, or even the elaborate structures of symbols through which the reader's vision is forced to deepen from social to metaphysical levels. One does not have to know her comments on Hawthorne and romance to recognize that the often extreme stylization of her work suggests allegory. In fact, anyone who has read more than a half-dozen of her stories will recognize recurring types and relations of characters, the common themes, the similarity of plot structures—all of which suggest that the literal is being manipulated for allegorical ends.

The second of her two main prescriptions shows that, at least in theory, she knew the dangers inherent in such allegory. She repeatedly warned students that stories do not begin with problems or issues that the writer feels a need to illustrate in some way; they begin with concrete situations, and the author's beliefs will determine *how* he sees the situation but they should not determine *what* he sees (*Mystery and Manners*, pp. 90–91). Thus, she cited the impressionistic Conrad ("before all, to make you *see*") as often as she did the allegorical Hawthorne. There seems to be a conflict here between the allegorist's use of the natural to signify something beyond it and the impressionist's concern for the natural itself. But for the Christian humanist this is a false conflict arising from a false dualistic understanding of existence, from an inability to see the whole horse. If one saw only half a horse (either spirit or matter) or, at best, a schizophrenic horse (of irreconcilable spirit and matter), one would not understand how anagogical vision reconciled allegory and impressionism. One would see allegory as only a rhetorical means of signifying the spiritual or of representing conceptions about the natural. One would not consider allegory as a way of seeing. For the anagogical writer, however, especially the writer whose religious faith is centered on the Incarnation, the natural and the supernatural contain each other; the different levels of meaning are intrinsic to the image. The allegory of such a writer is more than a technique of discourse; it is a way of seeing the concrete situation most fully. He does not try to find more meaning in the situation he creates, for that would suggest that the situation contained hidden kernels of meaning and that the reader's job was to husk the story to get the messages out of it—an attitude against which Miss O'Connor often warned her readers. Instead, the religious humanist writes allegory to see more of the situation. His task is extraordinarily difficult, since it requires a wholeness of vision which theologians have associated with prophecy and which literary critics, following Blake and Coleridge, have associated with the poetic imagination at its highest, with the ability to represent multëity in unity. Furthermore, such a writer will be distrusted by all sides since he will be too robustly profane for the religious idealist and too dogmatically spiritual for the naturalist who confounds skepticism with wisdom.

If Miss O'Connor's fiction is successfully anagogical, as her critical comments show she intended it to be, then some form of anagogical reading of it would be necessary. The reader who responded to a single level of meaning would be responding not only partially but wrongly; he would be denying her central assumptions about existence. For example, it would be a basic distortion not to realize that in her work to be estranged from God is necessarily to be estranged from one's essential self, which involves a form of psychological imbalance and neurotic compulsion. This spiritual and psychic estrangement also causes an estrangement from other men, thus some form of anti-social, or more precisely "anti-communal," behavior. These "levels of meaning" are actually not distinct levels at all; they become so only for the convenience of critical description; and as we assume temporarily the point of view of any one discipline, it must be to see more of the fictional work by moving around it and seeing it in new relationships. Thus, I hope to disclose more of Miss O'Connor's fiction by applying various disciplines in my interpretations, but I also hope to show that these disciplines are inseparable, that they are but different ways of talking about the fully integral universe of Miss O'Connor's fiction.

The assumption that I hope to substantiate through analysis of the works is that the fiction of a Christian humanist is best appreciated through a broadly humanistic approach. Romano Guardini, at least two of whose books Miss O'Connor read, has developed all of his work about a similar assumption: that "to view the pattern of Christian existence as a whole" one must resist the modern tendency to divide and isolate areas of knowledge. Like many Catholic writers, Guardini looks with some nostalgia to an earlier time when epistemological unity resulted from belief in ontological unity: "Early Christian thought had this universal view. Augustine draws no methodological division between philosophy and theology or, in philosophy, between metaphysics and psychology, within theology, between theoretical dogma and practical application to life but his mind proceeds from the whole of Christian existence to consider the total pattern and its different parts." [5] The direction in which such mental activity proceeds is important here. If one believes that existence is basically unified, one cannot adequately approach it from any one separate discipline. The mind must begin with the "whole of Christian existence" and move to the parts of the pattern: wisdom, which is supernatural, revealed, and universal, must precede understanding, which is natural and therefore partial. When Guardini writes of the "whole of Christian existence," he obviously is not using the term in a quantitative sense; he claims that the "universal view" apprehends existence not in all of its diversity, but in its essential unity. In Matthew Arnold's famous terms, it "sees life steadily and sees it whole." This issue is particularly important in Flannery O'Connor's work. Clearly, her range of subjects and themes is small. As many commentators have noted, there is much of life, even of particularly Christian life, that she does not consider. But the number and variety of objects that one sees does not determine the universality of vision. As she wrote about the aim of fiction, "the longer you look at one object, the more of the world you see in it; and it's well to remember that the serious fiction writer always writes about the whole world, no matter how limited his particular scene" (*Mystery and Manners*, p. 77). In this statement she adopts a position analogous to Guardini's; both assume that the essential unity of existence requires a wholeness of intellectual or artistic vision. Since he is a philosopher and a theologian and she is an artist, they differ in their specific concerns: he writes of a unity of intellectual disciplines subordinated to revelation, and she writes of a more immediate and concrete wholeness of imaginative experience as enlightened by faith. His disciplines tend to be analytical and abstract in their modes of operation, whereas she often stresses that fiction, both in the process of writing and the experience of reading, is neither of these and that it does not begin and should not end in reductive abstractions. One of the jobs of the literary critic, however, is to mediate between these different modes, to analyze the literary work while respecting its integrity. This means that the critic, if he is more interested in the literature than in his method, must not convert that literature into another discipline or even into several other disciplines. He must not assume that accumulating enough theological, philosophical, social, and psychological significances would explain the work. He must assume that these significances are not separable but that they each describe the wholeness of the author's vision while being themselves less than it. In this way the critic would be both analytic and synthetic: he would use analytic and intermediate approaches, but he would try to show that they converge in the integral vision. In a sense, he would try to demonstrate the multëity in unity of those types of significances, thus demonstrating both the extensiveness and the oneness of the author's view.

Thus far, I have suggested that this critical approach is justified, even required, by the basic assumptions from which Miss O'Connor wrote and by her faith. The demands are even stronger, however, because her respect for the whole horse not only affected the form of her fiction, giving it that strange combination of mystery and manners about which she has commented, but it also provided her most important themes. Above all—even above, because it includes, her preoccupations with original sin, grace, and freedom—she wrote about wholeness and incompleteness, subjects that are enormously complex and that, in various senses, will be the main concerns of this study. Reinhold Niebuhr, in giving his own rendering of the Catholic *justitia originalis*, provides a useful division of "this original righteousness which even sinful man has, not as a possession but in his sense of something lacking":

> It contains three terms: (a) The perfect relation of the soul to God in which obedience is transcended by love, trust, and confidence ("Thou shalt love the Lord thy God"); (b) the perfect internal harmony of the soul with itself in all of its desires and impulses: "With all thy heart and all thy soul and all thy mind"; and (c) the perfect harmony of life with life: "Thou shalt love thy neighbor as thyself." [6]

Although Niebuhr's Protestant emphasis in the first term falls rather heavily on faith and diminishes the importance of the Catholic concern with grace and its vehicles, his interpretation of man's original righteousness is suggestive, particularly since it is mainly concerned with the harmonies and relationships in wholeness. For the Catholic, this wholeness (the "terms" of which are merely different manifestations) was lost in the Fall but is vouchsafed to man through the sanctification of grace. Correspondingly, many modern theologians approach the question of sinfulness in terms of broken harmony, of estrangement or alienation. Tillich, for example, defines original sin in terms that complement Niebuhr's description of the *justitia originalis:* "estrangement from oneself, from the other man, from the ground out of which we come and to which we go." [7] It is quite possible, then, to use the general concepts of unity and estrangement as means of approaching the central Christian subjects of man's essential nature, his fallen state, and his redemption; and it is possible to use them to examine man from three perspectives, as a religious, psychological, and social being.

The first term of this question of wholeness—religious unity, the relationship of the creation to God, of the finite to the infinite—is the most obvious term in Flannery O'Connor's work, but it has also been one of the most controversial subjects among her critics. No commentators seemingly deny that Miss O'Connor overtly believed in the orthodox Catholic conceptions of existence, in the essential goodness of the creation and the immanence of God. In her essays and lectures she frequently opposed dualistic separation of nature and spirit, whether through Gnostic idealism or the radical Protestant's rejection of the world. Her emphasis on the Incarnation and sacramentalism are doctrinal centers for her more general belief that "this physical, sensible world is good because it proceeds from a divine source," and she associated this belief in the world's goodness with her artistic vocation: "The artist usually knows this by instinct; his senses, which are used to penetrating the concrete, tell him so" (*Mystery and Manners*, p. 157). This is not to say that the world is a sufficient end, which is concupiscent, or that it is valuable only as a product of the Creator, which is deistic; "the artist penetrates the concrete world in order to find at its depths the image of its source, the image of ultimate reality" (ibid.). Furthermore, this ultimate reality is not only a source in an historical sense, a prime mover in a chronological series of causes; it is the source in an eternal act of creation; it is the ground of all finite being; and, as Miss O'Connor wrote, it is contained in the natural even while infinitely transcending it.

A novelist who believes that the infinite is manifested in

the finite can have an even greater respect for created existence than can the naturalist. Although such a Christian humanist believes that the finite is not the totality of existence, that it is necessarily lacking, he also believes it to be more than the naturalist can admit to. He accepts its full temporal value, for he is not compelled to renounce the world in idealistic contempt, yet he also loves it for revealing a reality infinitely greater. Thus, the world is more for him than for the naturalist because it is less complete. This complexity, however, leads him into an apparent dilemma. If he loves the world more for its added dimension, he must also suffer the earthly deficiencies of which that dimension makes him aware. True, he can never see the world *sub specie aeternitatis*, he can never fully understand what the world is not; therefore, he has no right to be scornful by assuming an infinite perspective. Yet he can never be satisfied with the world, for he knows that between the finite and the infinite there is a difference greater than he can understand. The naturalist does not have this dilemma, for he has cut the losses he risks with his perspective. (This "naturalist" is hypothetical; as I intend to show in the next chapter, Miss O'Connor, like Kierkegaard, implies the impossibility of a complete naturalist.) The naturalist may be dissatisfied with present earthly existence. He may see the world as deteriorating from a mythical golden age; he may anticipate, or at least desire, a secular millennium, such as Marx's classless society, Norman O. Brown's uninhibited sensuous culture, the hippies' anarchy of love and individualism; he may cynically assume that the world cannot be what he could imagine as perfection. But in any of these cases his conception of the perfect is derived from the world as it is. The differences are quantitative —more altruism, more creativity and freedom, less hatred and aggressiveness. For the Christian, however, the difference between the world and God is qualitative. The world, by reason of its finitude, its creatureliness, is distinct from God. However, if this distinction were complete, there would be no dilemma; the Christian, as a Gnostic or Manichae, would be almost a mirror image of the naturalist, either despairing or seeking God through mysticism, mortification, and death. But the Christian humanist believes that the difference, although infinite, is not complete. Since God is the ground of all being, the world could be entirely separated from Him only by ceasing to be. The Christian humanist also believes that even man's attempts to deny or defy God cannot destroy the infinite within him.

This issue of defiance introduces yet other complexities in the Christian humanist's dilemma, the problem of sin and the Fall. So far we have treated the dilemma of religious unity from a generally Neo-Platonic point of view, as if the problem of separation involved only the distinction between creator and creation. But man complicates the problem because he has the ability to turn from God by free acts of his will. Nonhuman nature is innocent because it is not free, because it is bound by the necessities of natural law. But man is free, for he is a spiritual creature, and in this freedom he is both more divine and more capable of separation from God. Man is more glorious and more grotesque than the rest of creation, more grotesque because in his sinfulness he further removes himself from the source of his being and further destroys his essential self; he continuously defaces the image of God in which he is made. Thus, although unity with God is man's central, if unrecognized, desire, this unity cannot be complete. Man is an awkward amphibian of spirit and nature. Even when open to grace he is not perfected; as Flannery O'Connor wrote about the good, "Few have stared at that long enough to accept the fact that its face too is grotesque, that in us the good is something under construction" (*Mystery and Manners*, p. 226).

These humanistic dilemmas seem to be largely responsible for the charges that Miss O'Connor, like Milton, was of the devil's party without realizing it. Most recently Irving Malin has elaborated John Hawkes's earlier comments on the ambiguity between the Christian believer and the satanic writer. Malin claims, "She must believe *as a Christian* in free will and spiritual design. But *as a writer* she reinforces the grotesquerie of existence." This claim is similar to the suspicion of other commentators that Miss O'Connor had a strong element of Manicheism or Jansenism, but it manages to spare her as a Christian by finding only her artistic temperament to be heretical. In making this distinction it suggests that, while she consciously believed in the goodness of creation and the freedom of man, her fiction reveals that she unconsciously believed the opposite.[8]

Since these claims are primarily concerned with Miss O'Connor's characters and since other writers have demonstrated well that the world in her work is, in Hopkins' phrase, "charged with the grandeur of God," we can limit the issue to her attitude toward mankind. I find it surprising that critics who have found irreconcilable conceptions of man in her work have not paid more attention to the story "A Temple of the Holy Ghost," where such conflicts are not only explicit but are the thematic centers of the story. It is a bit disheartening to sneak around to the back of an author's mind to discover how she really feels about things, only to find her there already, not only aware of what she is doing but fully in control of it. But perhaps we should be more wary of the residual Freudian assumption that the unconscious gesture is the most true, especially when that assumption leads to ingenious attempts to outwit the fiction writer for the sake of critical insight.

The central theme of the story is Paul's teaching that man is a temple of the living God. No matter how deformed in body or soul, he is a habitation of the Spirit. The theme is developed primarily through the discoveries of a twelve-year-old girl who, in a symbolic initiation into adulthood, learns that this lesson applies even to a sideshow hermaphrodite, who becomes associated with the sacramental presence of Christ in the Host. As is often the case with Miss O'Connor's fiction, however, such a brief statement of theme seriously distorts the work, in itself a good indication of how fully concrete her fiction is. First, the story is not as sentimental as the moral ("We are all God's children") suggests. In fact, the authorial tone and the characterizations produce a strongly complementary theme: although man is a temple of the Holy Ghost, he certainly is grotesque. All of the characters are comic to some extent, whether physically ludicrous like the two-hundred-fifty-pound, sweaty, hairy, eighteen-year-old Alonzo Myers, or socially ludicrous like the prim and obtuse spinster, Miss Kirby, or emotionally ludicrous like the giggling, vain, adolescent convent girls. Even those characters who present the most valid religious points of view are comic. The most obvious example is Sister Perpetua, who introduced the main symbol of the story by advising the girls that if a young man should "behave in an ungentlemanly manner with them in the back of an automobile," they should put an end to it by saying, "Stop, Sir! I am a Temple of the Holy Ghost!" [9] Although the fourteen-year-old girls are shallow in all thing spiritual and nervously silly in most things sexual, nevertheless these children of this world are wiser in their generation than dear naive Sister Perpetua, the oldest nun in the convent. When the twelve-year-old visits the convent later in the story, we are presented briefly with another of the Sisters of Mercy, a "big moon-faced nun," who misses one opportunity to embrace the child but who wins in a surprise attack: "As they were leaving the convent door, the big nun swooped down on her mischievously and nearly smothered her in the black habit, mashing the side of her face into the crucifix hitched onto her belt and then holding her off and looking at her with little periwinkle eyes" (p. 100). The nun's actions come from affection and goodness, but they are still comically tinged by the physical and emotional clumsiness of being human. The slight ambivalence toward such characters shows that the author believes man to be an amphibious creature: on the one hand, the image of God, the temple of the Holy Ghost, an infinite and divine being; on the other hand, a defaced image, a ruined temple, a grotesque freak, continuously mutilating the divine image through his pride and feelings of self-sufficiency.

Clearly, Miss O'Connor's use of the grotesque involves judgment. It describes a deficiency, a deviation from an ideal of human perfection, from the image of God. Yet the attitudes in such judgment can be complex, especially since the author knows that we all share the state of the freak (which does not call for sentimental compassion any more than it calls for self-righteousness). A nun with a mischievous affection, a couple of silly adolescents, a farmer who runs a taxi service for Negro farmhands when he goes courting are not scorned with savage indignation. They are instead enjoyed as much as, or more than, they are exposed. Frequently her "satire" is closer to the humor that Romano Guardini praises as "a wonderful thing, the humor of a religious man who carries everything into the boundless love of God, including the inadequate, the strange, the queer." [10] That religious man does not pretend that the inadequate is adequate, the strange is familiar, or the queer is normal, for he is not compelled to the falsely generous blindness in which one ignores reality and calls one's forced ignorance "love." In contrast, since he is truly capable of love, he can accept man in his fallen state without scorn or arrogance.

Miss O'Connor's complex attitudes toward amphibious man are shown well in the two most important characters in this story. The sideshow freak is a symbol of man's natural deformity and a reminder that deformed man is still a temple of the Holy Ghost. Yet Miss O'Connor does not sentimentalize the character or simplify the ambiguities of the symbol. As the freak admits, he is "making the best" of his condition, which means that he is capitalizing on the deformity itself and on his customers' fascination with the sexually bizarre. If one were to extend the interpretation into tenuously detailed allegory, one might even suggest that the freak's statement, "This is the way He wanted me to be and I ain't disputing His way" (p. 97), reveals that fallen man shifts the responsibility for his nature to God and then exploits his fallen condition without feeling guilt. Such exploitation does not invalidate the child's epiphany which is stimulated by an account of the freak, however, nor does it justify the preachers who shut down the fair, presumably because they are shocked at seeing unaccommodated man. Miss O'Connor's use of the symbol is ironic, but her irony is not its own end, nor is it the endlessly dialectic irony of the skeptic.

Finally, the twelve-year-old girl through whom most of the story is seen best illustrates the religious complexity of mankind in Miss O'Connor's view. The girl's attitudes toward religion are a combination of devotion, awe, pride, and pre-adolescent fantasy. Her Catholicism enables her revelation, but it also makes her feel superior to the Baptist preacher she imitates and to the "big dumb Church of God ox" who thinks the *Tantum ergo Sacramentum* must be "Jew singing." Although her daydream about being a Christian martyr is connected with the fine perception that being a saint is the one vocation that includes everything, it also has much in common with her fantasy about being a World War II fighter pilot. Her experiences centered on the freak are, in one sense, true religious epiphanies in her symbolic confirmation; but, in another sense, they are associated with the girl's age and emotional perplexities. The use of the hermaphrodite as the central object of religious mystery suggests that the girl's experiences are partly the confused beginnings of sexual initiation, particularly since the story contains so many references to sexuality: the two convent girls' preoccupation with boys, the child's puzzlement that the freak can be a man and a woman without having two heads, her promise to tell about a rabbit's giving birth (by spitting babies out of its mouth), and her war fantasy in which she warns her fellow pilots that she would court-martial them before they could marry her. Miss O'Connor's use of sexuality does not mean that she is psychologically explaining away religious epiphanies. Such an approach assumes that the lowest, rather than the highest, common denominator most fully explains experiences. Instead, she is demonstrating that religious mysteries and illuminations have their consequences, parallels, and even partial (although hardly sufficient) causes in the natural world.[11] This demonstration itself proceeds from the central belief that I have been discussing, that existence is a whole with interpenetrations of the natural and the supernatural. It also derives from the complementary belief that while man is divine, he is infinitely different from God and is thus a grotesque and comic creature. Even his revelations are inseparable from his perplexing animal nature. So associating religious confirmation and sexual discovery (which is hardly strange to the anthropologist) is both mysterious and radically comic (does man know which end is up?). The philosophical monist or the dualist might assume attitudes of either awe or comic amusement toward this association, but only the Christian humanist is capable of both attitudes at once.

Thus far, I have considered the first term of man's wholeness and incompleteness, man's relation to God in terms of man's finitude and infinitude, but in doing so I have necessarily touched upon the other terms. One cannot completely separate the religious, psychological, and social perspectives, for they are merely three different contexts in which to see the same subject. For the Christian humanist, the first term, the metaphysical conception of man as a synthesis of the finite and infinite, is fundamental to any other approach. The other two terms of analysis begin with this religious conception and extend it into psychological and social contexts.

According to this view, if man is in a proper relation to God—the necessary term for any stable wholeness of being—he also has what Niebuhr called "the perfect internal harmony of the soul with itself in all of its desires and impulses"; he has psychological wholeness. In a frequently quoted statement, Miss O'Connor said that "to be able to recognize a freak, you have to have some conception of the whole man," and she then identified the whole man as the image of God and the freak in literature as "a figure for our essential displacement" (*Mystery and Manners*, pp. 44–45). These associations suggest that she based her conception of the man who is not whole, even though he may be a man of many parts, upon the commonly modern conception of estrangement, estrangement from God and from man's essential self, which is the image of God. Thus, if the Christian humanist considers psychological problems inseparable from religious ones, the discussion of the second term, of man's relation to his self, must return to the previous discussion of man's relation to God, but from a different point of view.

In *The Sickness Unto Death*, Kierkegaard begins his analysis of the self with the ontological assumption that I have been discussing, that man is a synthesis, and from it he derives the most impressive religious psychology since St. Thomas. The assumption hardly originates with Kierkegaard, but the perceptiveness with which he explores it makes him the most influential psychologist among modern theologians and religious philosophers. He defines the self as "a relation which relates itself to its own self"; [12] that is, a relation between the finite and infinite, temporal and eternal, corporeal and spiritual, which conceives of its own identity yet is separate from that identity (or it could not relate to it). The fully restricting clause, "which relates itself to its own self," is the basis of existentialism, whether theistic or atheistic. Reinhold Niebuhr, for example reproduces it when he claims, "Man is the only animal which can make itself its own object. This capacity for self-transcendence which distinguishes spirit in man from soul (which he shares with animal existence), is the basis of discrete individuality, for this self-consciousness involves consciousness of the world as the 'other.' " [13] Sartre, too, reproduces it in his major concept that man is the only earthly being whose essence is not identical with its existence, who is "being-for-itself" rather than "being-in-itself," and who thus has freedom, self-consciousness, and in effect, self-transcendence. For Kierkegaard, Niebuhr, and Sartre, man is more than any conception of himself that he can formulate; as a "self" he is more than he can be as an "object." To be free and fully human he must be self-conscious, but he must not attempt to reduce his self to the image he has conceived, to transform his changing self into a fixed existence, or he will destroy his internal harmony.

Usually, however, man is afraid of being free; and so he tries to destroy his selfhood, which means that he must destroy his wholeness, his humanity, and, therefore, his proper relation to God. For the Christian psychologist, this means that man attempts to deny the essential self from which he has fallen and to substitute a more limited conception of what he is. He tries to believe that there was no Fall, that his present state is his essential one, that he is not estranged. But since he cannot entirely destroy his original essence, his attempts to reduce the self to the finite make him more estranged, divided, and self-defeating. He becomes less capable of performing what Paul Tillich calls "a total and centered act of the personality, an act in which all the drives and influences which constitute the destiny of man are brought into the centered unity of a decision."[14] He becomes less self-controlled, more neurotic; he feels ill at ease with himself, and, despite his insistent claim to self-knowledge, he is repeatedly disturbed by those impulses which do not fit his theories and which he cannot control. As Erich Fromm has written, paralleling Tillich, the alienated person "experiences himself as an alien." He has become "estranged from himself. He does not experience himself as the center of his world, as the creator of his own acts—but his acts and their consequences have become his masters, whom he obeys, or whom he may even worship."[15] Although Fromm's concern is primarily with cultural determinants and solutions, his description of the psychological state is similar to the theologians' account of sinfulness as estrangement from an unfallen, essential nature.

I shall explore further the causes and form of such estrangement in Flannery O'Connor's work, but here I shall only suggest its importance by pointing out that her stories usually climax in a character's suddenly expanded self-awareness. Characters who felt that they knew themselves and their worth recognize desires, fears, and even destructive impulses that their self-conceptions had forcefully hidden. They realize that even those proud self-conceptions were created from the neurotic needs of their estrangement. Quite often these climaxes occur in a sudden recognition of the irrational. Sometimes the irrational is the truly mysterious within man; it is behavior that cannot be fully explained in terms of natural causes, and it shows that man is more than his theories can encompass or limit. Whether it is a gesture of unmotivated evil or of senseless love, it signifies the remains of freedom and the possibility that he is futilely trying to deny. In other cases, the irrational may show man's bondage, the compulsiveness that comes from his lack of psychological harmony. In this sense, in recognizing his irrationality, the character realizes his fallen state.

Finally, to connect these concepts with religious unity, one must remember that man's estrangement from his essential self, his whole, unfallen, eternal self, is necessarily estrangement from God. To the Christian humanist, since God is the ground of man's being, the center of his essential self, He is not the "other," not what Blake attacked as the completely external Nobbodaddy; He is the "Centre of centres." When one works from this point of view and explores the psychological correspondences, one finds new meaning in the basic Christian belief that man's freedom is obtained in accepting the will of God, his bondage in rebellion. Miss O'Connor worked from such beliefs to show the demons of the mind by which man enslaves himself and the means of salvation by which he is freed and made whole.

The third and final term of man's wholeness, "the perfect harmony of life with life," is impossible to achieve without the other terms. Thus, any attempt to establish a social, political, and economic utopia that does not consider man's relation to God and to himself is necessarily blind, for it tries to manipulate man without a sufficient conception of his nature and condition. The Christian humanist, above all, must reject a sociology that is entirely separated from other disciplines, including theology. He must refuse to consider man exclusively as a social animal, even for the limited purpose of producing a workable social structure. To limit excessively one's conception of man for expedience must eventually be inexpedient, for one cannot determine necessary means without an adequate conception of the ends to be served. An awareness of this problem, by naturalists as well as theists, has lately produced strong criticism of both capitalistic and Marxian economics, of pragmatic, regressive educational systems, of mass collectives, and of vastly complex social machines that dehumanize man to produce more efficiently a Midas' wealth.

Ernest Becker considers a reductive conception of other men to be analogous to fetishism, wherein the sexually neurotic person concentrates his desire on a part of another because he is psychologically unable to encounter the whole person. Although Becker points out that almost all of man's cultural life involves some fetishism (since "total encounters" are impossible in all social relations), he claims convincingly that fearful, neurotic people are more strongly compelled to reduce other people to objects that are easier to understand and respond to.[16] Thus, the man who is estranged from himself is necessarily estranged from others; only the whole man can psychologically afford to see other men as whole, and only he can fully love.

The natural organization of fetishistic or socially estranged men is the collective, the association of individuals for economic and political expediency. Since the collective is based upon a few practical common interests, particularly the production and consumption of goods, it reduces the necessary relationship between its members. So, Thomas Carlyle objected in the 1840s that industrial society was reducing human relationships to the "cash nexus," and so Teilhard de Chardin objected in the terms of his system of spiritual evolution that "so long as it absorbs or appears to absorb the person, collectivity kills the love that is trying to come to birth. As such collectivity is essentially unlovable. . . . It is impossible to give oneself to an anonymous number." [17] Both authors, from their very different points of view, believe that the collective cannot accommodate the whole man, the person as opposed to the individual, because its essentially materialistic purposes omit other dimensions. By contrast, the community is more integral; its relationships are more varied and personal, its origins more traditional and organic. It is something to which one belongs, rather than a place where one is; and it assumes that man is more than an adjustable machine, for it accepts the irrational and the personal.

As many critics have noted, Flannery O'Connor persistently represents cities as the domain of the devil (with similarities to Sodom and Gomorrah and to Augustine's earthly city), as a nightmare world, and as an insipid place full of lonely or flat people. Correspondingly, in keeping with the Southern agrarian tradition, she often represents the farm as a place of complex and deep loyalties, where one feels related to the land and one's work and where the relations between people are vitally important and therefore elaborately formalized through manners. The difference is essentially the contrast between the urban collective and the rural community. Miss O'Connor does show at times that attachment to the farm can be a form of estrangement, an attempt to reduce one's concerns within manageable limits and find a hiding place. But more often she uses it to suggest greater complexities of being or the greater possibility for completeness or even the greater difficulty of man's pretending that he is already complete.

Significantly, Miss O'Connor's characters are often displaced from their communities. Sometimes they are geographically displaced like the old men of "The Geranium" and "Judgment Day," who long to escape from the Northern city and return to the Southern countryside. Sometimes they journey from their country homes to the city, like Hazel Motes and Francis Tarwater of the two novels or Mr. Head and Nelson in "The Artificial Nigger." Sometimes they are chronologically displaced, like the Grandmother in "A Good Man Is Hard to Find," who dreams of her childhood and talks of better times, or the mother and son in "Everything That Rises Must Converge," who look back to a time when their family was prominent. These displacements are important socially as manifestations of destroyed or decaying human community, but they are also important as symbols of man's spiritual and psychological estrangements, as images of a lost Eden which he still vaguely remembers because the image of God has not been entirely defaced. And, finally, they can be partially sentimental dreams, a simplification by which the characters try to substitute one aspect of their lost wholeness for the entire state, by which they try to reduce their displacement from God to a geographical or historical matter.

To avoid this mistake of confusing one symptom of estrangement with the entire disease, one must try to comprehend the diversity and unity of existence while still recognizing his limits, still preserving a sense of mystery. This means, above all, that one must respect Allen Tate's whole horse in all of its dimensions, which requires that one see not only the whole of the horse but also the horse as a whole. Flannery O'Connor does so. As a Christian humanist with an intense concern for art as well as for faith, she presents man in his relationships to God, to himself, and to other men, and she reveals that all of these relationships are indivisible aspects of his being. Thus, even as she shows the many ways in which man tries to destroy his essential, whole self, she also shows that those attempts can never entirely succeed; the very interrelationships of his motives indicate that the whole self cannot be completely destroyed and that man remains free enough to be healed.

2. Demons and Neuroses

$\mathcal{I}f$ the whole man is a synthesis of the divine and the earthly, and if all men retain something of this wholeness, then all men are, to some extent, free. If man were able to cast away his divinity, he could become an entirely natural being, determined by natural law; psychology could completely replace ethics, since man could not be responsible for his actions and no act could be judged as good in itself, as having any value apart from natural expediency. But the Christian humanist cannot admit the complete loss of divinity, for man would cease to be man if he were not a synthesis, which is the essence of his being. In the common terms of modern theology, man must be "a living limit" and a "relation"; he must exist "at the boundary"; thus, he must be free because he cannot escape possibility. And to be free, as existentialism has taught religious psychology, is to be in dread. I need not discuss this connection, for it has been perhaps the most popular subject of existentialism; it is enough to mention that dread, or *angst*, indicates man's greatness, his divinity and freedom.

Being in dread, man has two general alternatives from the

31

Christian humanist's point of view. He can accept himself, his limitations, his freedom, his responsibility, and his proper relation to God; that is, he can accept grace and have faith. Or he can sin, which is to turn from God and to deny his essential self, to try to escape from dread through his own resources. For the Christian humanist the attempt to escape dread through sin is wrong, not only because it is evil, but also because it is error, which must make the sinful man ultimately self-defeating. Thus, turning from God is more than an ethical problem; it manifests itself in every aspect of man's being. Similarly, a number of psychologists, particularly Adlerians, have claimed that neurosis comes mainly from insecurity, particularly as it manifests itself in the compensatory will-to-power by which man tries to obscure his feelings of inferiority. Even Freud's theory of the death wish suggests that a feeling of incompleteness is fundamental to neurotic self-assertion: since the individual longs to escape his incompleteness, his unfulfillable and Faustian desires (which many theologians associate with man's divinity), he wishes for nirvana or death; the life-wish, however, directs this primal masochism outward as sadism. The religious psychologist finds value in both of these theories, for he too believes that sinful man's neuroses result mainly from his insecurity and from an incompleteness he never can entirely accept. The theist, however, does not believe that man's insecurity has primarily environmental or biological causes (although these may be involved); for him, insecurity is basic to man's nature as a free, spiritual-corporeal being, and neuroses are mainly the psychological accompaniments of the attempts to escape insecurity, or dread, through sin.

Since human freedom depends on man's dual nature, his attempts to escape the anxiety of freedom usually involve his denying one of the two terms of that nature. He may reject his finitude and try to become one with God, the way of the Christian mystic or the Hindu. Such attempts have been discussed by de Rougemont and D'Arcy as Manichean heresies, socially destructive forces, and self-sacrificial perversions of agape.[1] Although such flights from the self may be important through various sublimated forces, in their overt forms they have not been Western man's primary means of escape. Instead, he usually tries to deny the divine within himself and tries to live entirely within the finite. This does not mean that he succeeds in becoming an atheist. As Tillich claims, genuine atheism is impossible since man replaces God with other gods, since he establishes something finite (human love, the state, pleasure, progress, etc.) as his ultimate concern.[2] So, he is not a secularist, but an idolater. Tillich has made this concept most famous through his discussion of the "demonic"; in both Old and New Testament usages, men who worship idols and follow strange gods are possessed by demons, by "structures of evil" that are inevitably destructive. The man who turns from God must become demonic, for he must continuously cast the eternal from himself by maintaining a finite object of worship, even if he is not aware of the god which his order serves. This turning from God is not a single and conclusive act but a continual process; as Kierkegaard claims, to be in the despair of estrangement is continuously to contract it.[3] Thus, demonic activity must be a sustained flight from dread and freedom, a sustained and compulsive denial of reality; but, since the object of worship is finite, it is not adequate to support its deification, and it must fail the worshipper, returning him to the anxiety that has always been haunting him just outside the edge of his neurotically limited attention.

Flannery O'Connor's characters who have turned from God correspond quite closely to this general description of the demonic and its causes. Too often it is carelessly assumed that Miss O'Connor begins her story with godless people who have become quite comfortable with themselves and that she then has God suddenly illumine them by removing the scales from their eyes and forcing them to look at themselves. Although there is some truth to this criticism, it greatly oversimplifies her conception of estranged, demonic man, and it thus oversimplifies the mode by which grace operates through nature in the stories. Her characters are very seldom at ease with themselves or their circumstances, even though they often insist upon their blessings. They are troubled by vague anxieties which they usually try to fix onto comprehensible and even controllable objects, and they have established ritualistic acts by which they try to protect themselves from what they fear. Their actions are futile, however, since the objects of their fear are merely counters for a more existential dread, and their rituals are compulsive holding actions against a reality from which they cannot indefinitely hide. Thus, if grace does come, it is not as God's ravishment; grace is always offered, but the characters can accept it only when their demonic defenses, which are tenuously and nervously held, finally collapse under natural circumstances.

Mrs. Cope, in "A Circle in the Fire," is a complete example of the pattern. In the deepest levels of her being she is in dread, which must have no specific object or it would be rational fear: "when the seasons changed she seemed almost frightened at her good fortune in escaping whatever it was that pursued her" (*Good Man*, p. 150). Perhaps the best explanation of her state comes at the end of the story when her farm has been set afire by Powell, a vicious, displaced boy from an Atlanta housing project. In her misery her face "looked as if it might have belonged to anybody, a Negro or a European or to Powell himself" (p. 154). Like all of mankind, Mrs. Cope is a vulnerable, displaced creature, and she builds her defenses against that fact. Appropriately, Miss O'Connor provides no other explanation. In some stories she gives a few more psychological insights into the reasons that the dread manifests itself as it does, but she never tries to explain the primary state itself. As she often stated in her lectures, the fiction writer takes us beyond the point that the psychologist, sociologist, or economist can account for. Miss O'Connor is most deeply concerned with the mystery in all men, which is not to say that she refuses authorial responsibility by claiming man to be a puzzling creature; rather, she finds that ultimate questions of human personality cannot be answered through natural determinants but must be considered theologically and metaphysically. Beneath the individual's psychological problems there is the problem of man, of his essence and his universal condition; when Miss O'Connor writes about a semi-allegorical Everyman, she is writing from the belief that man has an essential self and that his individual self cannot be understood apart from it. In associating Mrs. Cope with other suffering people, Miss O'Connor is both declaring the woman's commonality with the rest of mankind and suggesting the general state from which Mrs. Cope has fled and to which she is returned through suffering.

Fiction, however, cannot be concerned only with essences; mystery must be embodied in manners, and men in the state of dread make the "qualitative leaps" by which they establish their individual personalities. At such levels psychological and social questions become relevant. Mrs. Cope, a small, trim woman with neat flowerbeds, creates her defenses through her prosperous farm, her sense of decency, her vague, nearly impersonal pity for the "less fortunate," and her frequent insistence that she has much to be thankful for. For the most part, she has even managed to restrict her anxiety to problems like the weeds in her gardens ("She worked at the weeds and nut grass as if they were an evil sent directly by the devil to destroy the place" [pp. 130–31]) or her lazy Negroes ("Her Negroes were as destructive and impersonal as the nut grass" [p. 132]). Reducing the nature of the satanic to nut grass corresponds to her demonic elevation of the farm to blessedness, and considering her Negroes' laziness to be destructive similarly corresponds to her limiting virtue to industriousness and respectability. In constricting her universe she manages to confine her view of goodness and evil, salvation and damnation, God and the devil. She also tries to control destiny in two apparently similar but ultimately contradictory ways; directly, by her hard work at pulling weeds and watchfully managing the Negroes and, indirectly, by showing that she is one of the earthly elect and thus protected by supernatural forces. In a kind of secular Calvinism she insists that she is especially blessed and that she has good fortune. The contradiction implied here is also central to the Puritan ethic, which has frequently been discussed in psychological and social terms. In one way, Mrs. Cope believes that she can control things herself ("I have the best kept place in the country and do you know why? Because I work. I've had to work to save this place and work to keep it" [p. 134]). In another way, she fears that she is powerless, subject to the whims of fortune; this is particularly shown in her obsessive fear that fire will destroy the woods or that someone will get hurt on the property and sue her. In this regard, her hard work has irrational purposes; it is to show that she is chosen by fortune or at least worthy of being chosen. All Christians are concerned with the problem of human power and human powerlessness before God, but in her attempt to escape dread Mrs. Cope has thoroughly confounded self-determination and destiny; and while fearing her own impotence, she has tried to control things entirely.

Mrs. Cope's dilemma can also be approached through what Kierkegaard describes as the pagan's concept of fate, which is actually the "nothing of dread." Kierkegaard claims that the genius, the man of immediacy, subjectivity, and power that has not been posited as spirit, discovers fate as his limit, as the external determinant that he cannot predict or control, that is absolute but blind.[4] Although with her platitudes and carefully circumscribed views Mrs. Cope is hardly a genius, within her small domain she has the basic qualities of Kierkegaard's pagan hero. She is the successful ruler; she is an "omnipotent in-itself," relying on her own powers; yet she has a troubled awareness of an external power which she posits negatively as that which she cannot control; she is a very small and tidy genius with an unusually large fear. In fact, one might even suggest that her feelings of power and superiority, combined with her fear of an imminent, unknown destroyer, are generally paranoiac, at least to the extent that Kierkegaard's "genius" exemplifies a kind of cultural paranoia, which, as modern man well demonstrates, seems to be the most common neurosis of the man who tries to escape dread through his own will-to-power.

Mrs. Cope's fears, however, are far from entirely neurotic. They also indicate her defaced wholeness and show the possibility of her salvation. Kierkegaard said that the greater the genius, the more he discovers fate, since fate is "merely the anticipation of providence." Mrs. Cope's anxious concern with good fortune and trouble shows both a promising insecurity amidst her defenses and a naturalistic awareness of providence. If the spirit could be posited, Kierkegaard claimed, providence would also be posited and dread and fate would be annulled. This statement is similar to Guardini's claim that "once a man believes in Christ, Providence takes the place of destiny in directing his existence. This brings him by means of grace into the relation existing between the Father and the Incarnate Son. . . . In place of the mysterious, impersonal force conceived as destiny there appears the person of the Father." [5] Since God is not an impersonal force and not a complete other (as is fate), man would then not feel helpless and controlled by an arbitrary force that threatens to burn his woods. He could thus overcome both his neurotic obsessions and the existential dread that lies behind them. But to do so he must posit the spirit which he dedicatedly denies and accept the God he fears, which requires that he abandon his defensive self-sufficiency; otherwise, he would never be capable of relationship, and whatever is not himself would be the dreadful other.

Throughout "A Circle in the Fire" Mrs. Cope is confronted with examples of man's incompleteness, but she refuses to understand their significances or to admit their relevance to herself. She refuses to admit her kinship with the freak. In the opening pages Mrs. Pritchard, the hired woman, is established in comic contrast to the farm's owner as gossipy, suspicious, vulgar, and, above all, morbidly fascinated by the calamities that Mrs. Cope dislikes hearing about ("Mrs. Cope always changed the subject to something cheerful" [p. 131]). Although juxtaposing these characters makes them ludicrous through contrast, it also hints at their basic similarity. Both women are obsessed with calamity, but they control their obsessions in complementary ways, Mrs. Cope by pretending that the calamitous does not exist and Mrs. Pritchard by making an avocation of it. ("Mrs. Pritchard would go thirty miles for the satisfaction of seeing anybody laid away" [p. 131].) [6] Although Mrs. Pritchard is not developed psychologically but is used mainly as a foil, her gloomy predictions and feelings of superiority over the sufferers suggest that she, too, has found defenses for dealing with the irrational. Mrs. Cope cannot admit the other woman is a mirror image of herself, but when she is exasperated with her bespectacled tomboy daughter, she blurts out, "Sometimes you look like you might belong to Mrs. Pritchard" (p. 150). Beneath the contempt and condescension, the irony points to the kinship between the women. Even the spunkiness and comically violent imagination of the young daughter, one of Miss O'Connor's familiar fat twelve-year-old girls with braces, suggest the inadequacy of Mrs. Cope's attempt to keep everything genteel and bland.

The most obvious challenge to her forced complacency is the three young boys from the housing development. Although she tries to be "nice" to them, to isolate herself from them by pity and condescension, and to convince herself that they are young gentlemen who would never swear or set their younger brothers afire in a box, they increasingly impose themselves and terrify her with their irrational maliciousness. (Mrs. Cope's ridiculous pity for these "less fortunate" boys indicates that a sociological approach will not get us to the bottom of their evil.) In a suggestive expression of their passion and orneriness, the boys ride the forbidden horses, apparently being thrown in the process, and let the bull out of his pen. Both incidents suggest the lawless, even animalistic, vitality of the boys as it begins to break up the forms that Mrs. Cope has established for her life. Finally, they set fire to her woods, bringing upon her the fate she has feared and the providential humbling that she has not known she desires or needs. "She stood taut, listening, and could just catch in the distance a few wild high shrieks of joy as if the prophets were dancing in the fiery furnace, in the circle the angel had cleared for them" (p. 154). And in her misery she resembles those she has pitied, even the leader of the three boys.[7]

Since the farm is the main symbol of Mrs. Cope's neurotic and demonic flight, her attitudes toward it are necessarily complex. Early in the story she said, " 'Think of all we have. Lord,' she said and sighed, 'we have everything,' and she looked around at her rich pastures and hills heavy with timber and shook her head as if it might all be a burden she was trying to shake off her back" (p. 133). Allegorically, her possessions are burdensome as wealth that she unconsciously desires to cast from her; they are "rich" and "heavy," like the flesh of the concupiscent man who is not at ease with his or the world's body since he forces on them more significance than they can hold and is continuously exploiting them in symbolic gestures. Also, because Mrs. Cope has elevated her farm to an ultimate concern, has deified the finite, she must continuously fight religious wars against everything that would threaten the farm to any extent. Thus, as is characteristic of the neurotic, she lacks a sense of proportion regarding anything concerning her obsessions. When she pulls the weeds "as if they were an evil sent directly by the devil to destroy the place," she is not merely being energetic and conscientious; she is symbolically fighting off an attack on the sacred. It is quite vexing to have to protect such a vulnerable deity, as is usually shown when man mistakes the conditional for the unconditional. Finally, Mrs. Cope unconsciously needs to feel that her farm is a burden. As the saying goes, it keeps her mind off other things. This need, too, is a neurotic symptom: it is the neurotic's need for phobias so that he can reassure himself that what he fears is definable and fixed. As the Judge in "The Displaced Person" used to say, "The devil you know is better than the devil you don't" (*Good Man*, p. 216).

In "The Displaced Person," Miss O'Connor created another haunted character, Mrs. McIntyre, who also deifies her farm, but this character has a different syndrome to handle her anxiety. Whereas Mrs. Cope is wont to "recite a litany of her blessings," to give thanks for her good fortune, and to pity others, Mrs. McIntyre recites a litany of her troubles, believes that she owes nothing, and complains repeatedly about the Negroes, white-trash tenants, and "incidental bloodsuckers" who have misused her. Yet her complaining of struggle and poverty serves basically the same purposes as Mrs. Cope's gratefulness: it reduces the unknown to the known, the whole to a part. For Kierkegaard this is the essence of philistinism, which, trying to "tranquilize itself in the trivial" and being devoid of imagination, "carries possibility around like a prisoner in the cage of the probable, shows it off, imagines itself to be the master, does not take note that precisely thereby it has taken itself captive to be the slave of spiritlessness and to be the most pitiful of all things." [8] Miss O'Connor, who has described prophecy as a function of the imagination (rather than the moral sense) and as an act of seeing more in existence, is strongly aware of the captivity and pitifulness of philistinism. Mrs. McIntyre is, in her own limited sense, a good woman, a hard-working, honest, and fair landowner. In fact, she turns against her financial savior because she discovers that the displaced person intends to marry his white sixteen-year-old cousin to one of the Negro hands. Although she is somewhat worried that the thought of marrying a white woman will upset her Negroes, whom she needs on the farm, her reaction is mainly a moral and social revulsion ("What kind of a monster are you!"). Of course, the narrow and shallow morality is itself determined by her lack of vision. After she has discovered the D. P.'s intentions, she retires in despair to the roll-top desk which she has preserved as a memorial to her first husband; "It had been his first principle to talk as if he were the poorest man in the world and she followed it, not only because he had but because it was true. When she sat with her intense constricted face turned toward the empty safe, she knew there was nobody poorer in the world than she was" (p. 233). In her weariness and disgust with petty struggles, she senses her spiritual and emotional poverty. Apparently this had not always been so much the case. Although she married the Judge for his money, she liked the eccentric old man, even if she could not admit it to herself; but when he died, he left a bankrupt estate and the small farm that his widow struggled to preserve as her symbolic remnant of security.

Not all of Miss O'Connor's philistines are so obviously anxious. Some appear to have successfully tranquilized themselves in the trivial and in feelings of self-righteousness, but they still betray themselves by compulsive gestures or momentary doubts, showing why the defenses have been built and where they will fail. If one does not sense the importance of these gestures, the climactic revelations of the stories may seem arbitrary. "Revelation" has thus been criticized for ending with a religious vision "which the earlier development of the [story] does not justify." [9] Mrs. Turpin, the central character, sits in a doctor's waiting room, protected by her one-hundred-eighty pounds, her pride in being a small landowner, her good disposition, and her sense of decency and goodness. But, despite her insistent contentment, she is not really at ease with herself. Most importantly, she is too much bothered by the "white trash" in the room, too threatened by their laziness and self-possession, too compelled to rehearse her moral and social superiorities over them. She even feels scornful of the doctor's waiting room, which is hardly larger than a garage and which has limp magazines and a full ash tray on the table.

The only stranger in the room to whom she feels kinship is a well-dressed gray-haired lady who, with less social insecurity, condescends agreeably to Mrs. Turpin and the white trash. Furthermore, we find out that when Mrs. Turpin has trouble sleeping, she plays reassuring mental games such as "naming the classes of people" from colored people and white trash through homeowners to home-and-land owners like herself. Above her are just people with bigger houses and more land, people of her class but with more of the things she has. Yet even this game cannot completely cover her insecurity:

> But here the complexity of it would begin to bear in on her, for some of the people with a lot of money were common and ought to be below she and Claude and some of the people who had good blood had lost their money and had to rent and then there were colored people who owned their homes and land as well. There was a colored dentist in town who had two red Lincolns and a swimming pool and a farm with registered white-face cattle on it. Usually by the time she had fallen asleep all the classes of people were moiling and roiling around in her head, and she would dream they were all crammed in together in a box car, being ridden off to be put in a gas oven.[10]

This nightmare image of boxcars and concentration camps appears also in "A Circle in the Fire" and "The Displaced Person"; in all three stories it suggests, among other things, mankind's essential oneness and the characters' fear of the incomprehensible which pursues them, of whatever it is that they know they cannot control. Miss O'Connor's choice of the image is excellent. Although Hitler's fascism was horrifying in itself, it has become still more horrifying as a sign that man has not purged himself of the demonic. The gas ovens and secret police still serve our collective psyche, as do the symbols of nightmare. they stand for fears and self-knowledge so terrifying that they must be coded in the most terrifying public images we have. As the Victorian Englishman centered his anxiety on the fear of proletarian revolution, the twentieth-century man has centered his on fascism and more recently on

Communism and "the bomb." Thus, if Miss O'Connor's allusion to gas ovens might seem slightly too conscious in the case of Mrs. Turpin, it nevertheless suits the character's bourgeois representativeness. It suggests that no amount of social or psychological insularity can completely protect one from the common nightmares.

In the doctor's office Mrs. Turpin also feels defensive toward Mary Grace, the scowling daughter of the stylish lady. In retreat from the Wellesley girl's obvious dislike, Mrs. Turpin begins a mental counterattack. First, she tries pitying the girl for her acne-scarred face; then, as the girl's scowls turn to smirks, Mrs. Turpin places her among the inferior social orders: "What if Jesus had said, 'All right, you can be white-trash or a nigger or ugly'!" (p. 196). Above all, she feels that the girl has a bad disposition, which necessarily makes the girl's judgments unimportant.

So, when Mary Grace finally snaps, hits Mrs. Turpin with a copy of *Human Development*, tries to strangle the woman, and says to her, " 'Go back to hell where you came from, you old wart hog' " (p. 207), Mrs. Turpin is psychologically ready to begin her enlightenment, especially since the girl has spoken so pointedly to the situation, telling the pig farmer that even if you wash down a wart hog with a hose every day and keep it in a pig parlor, it is still a wart hog. The movement from the first shock to the final acceptance and vision is convincingly fitted to the earlier part of the story. Mrs. Turpin's repressed hostilities, the signs of insecurity that lay just beneath her good disposition, become more overt. Whereas she once routinely complained about "buttering up niggers," she now becomes openly angry at her ingratiating workers, and her previous irritation with the white trash, who have not been given her message, becomes hatred. Throughout, she has scorned anyone who would not show her the admiration she needed; so, now, feeling rejected by God, she begins to attack Him. Her beneficent Jesus has become her enemy, and in her "concentrated fury" she seems a warrior "going single-handed, weaponless, into battle." Without her psychological defenses she must confront a Jesus who is more than a reassuring echo of her self-righteousness; and becoming more and more resentful as she commands Him to justify her treatment, she finally blurts out the hysterical cry, " 'Who do you think you are?' " (p. 216). At last, she has gone too far to retreat into self-deception; she has revealed things about herself and her faith that she had never realized before. Harold Pinter once wrote that at some point in his plays his characters say something that they have never said before and that they cannot take back, something that they have been covering up by all their chatter.[11] This happens to Mrs. Turpin more clearly than to any other of Miss O'Connor's characters.

At this point the earth seems to expand suddenly, so that her husband's truck in the distance looks like a child's toy. She feels alone and vulnerable in a universe too vast to be controlled by her self-serving piety. Throughout her struggle to feel justified while accused, her surroundings have become religiously symbolic. When she returned to her farm, "she would not have been startled to see a burnt wound between two blackened chimneys" (p. 209). When she shook the hose with which she was washing down her hogs, "a watery snake appeared momentarily in the air" (p. 216). And, above all, infusing everything with its radiance, the sun has been transforming the earth, even suffusing the hogs with a red glow. In the context of this traditional symbolism, Mrs. Turpin's piety seems more than ever a parody of faith. Cut off from the essence of real love and humility, her feelings for Jesus have been egocentric and sentimental; she has loved a god created in her own image to fulfill her own needs. Unable any longer to sustain that image, she must admit her fearful littleness and her dependency on a God who is infinitely more than she is and who cannot be coerced by the cleanliness and grudging charities of his creatures. She is ready for her revelation.

As Mrs. Turpin is left with the quietness and the light of

the setting sun, she has a vision of the heavenly bridge on which "a vast horde of souls were rumbling toward heaven" (p. 217): white trash, niggers, freaks, lunatics, and finally the dignified respectable people whose virtues were being burned away. Perhaps the form of this vision is not quite appropriate to Mrs. Turpin. Especially as described with Miss O'Connor's irony and dexterity, it seems a bit too precise and clever, but who would wish to sacrifice that description for more stylistic realism? More importantly, the substance of the vision is quite justified by the structure and metaphorical development of the story (compare, for example, the masses of people in the box car with the "vast horde" of the saved) and by the development of the character. Miss O'Connor has achieved the difficult task of showing that grace works through nature without destroying it and that the acceptance of grace is both an appropriate and a free act. Miss O'Connor once described the climactic action of her stories in similar terms:

> I often ask myself what makes a story work, and what makes it hold up as a story, and I have decided that it is probably some action, some gesture of a character that is unlike any other in the story, one which indicates where the real heart of the story lies. This would have to be an action or a gesture which was both totally right and totally unexpected; it would have to be one that was both in character and beyond character; it would have to suggest both the world and eternity. (*Mystery and Manners*, p. 111)

To demand more justification than Miss O'Connor provides in this story is to demand psychological determinism and to deny that grace is freely given and freely accepted. It is to demand that the fully possible be imprisoned in the cage of the probable.

Despite their officiousness, Mrs. Cope, Mrs. McIntyre, and Mrs. Turpin all are in what Kierkegaard calls the despair of womanliness, of weakness, of not willing to be oneself.[12] They try to evade their selves by living in a spiritless world of objects, duties, and restricted conceptions of what they are. Although Miss O'Connor is frequently concerned with this kind of despair, perhaps because it is by far the most common form of the demonic, she also is an excellent interpreter of the complementary form, the despair of manliness, of willing to be oneself in despair. A person in such despair is the opposite of the philistine. He is intensely aware of the spiritual and of human possibilities for heroism and for suffering. He is introspective, concerned, above all, with realizing his infinite self. But he wills to be that self in complete disrelation to God, the ground of his essential being; thus, as Kierkegaard says, that which he wills to be is "only the abstractest possibility of self." Although he is more complex and more nearly complete than a Mrs. Cope or a Mrs. Turpin, he demonically worships a self that cannot be complete as long as he worships it. In one sense, he is more similar than the womanly despairer to the whole man, as Satan is more similar than man to the unfallen angels; but in another sense, he is farther from perfection, as Satan is more estranged than man from God. He who recognizes the eternal and opposes it has greater spirit and greater despair than the philistine.

Among characters in Miss O'Connor's short stories The Misfit in "A Good Man Is Hard to Find" is the most extensively developed character of this general type. One could approach this murderer from a clinically psychological point of view, for he has some classically psychotic symptoms. He has killed his father, an act which he cannot remember; he recoils violently when the Grandmother calls him one of her children and reaches out to touch him; he kills gratuitously and yet at times seems shy and embarrassed; and he feels dissociated from his crimes. Nevertheless, one could also approach him in terms of religious allegory. The patricide then symbolizes the rebellion of the Fall; the persistent punishment for unremembered crimes suggests the condition of man in original sin; The Misfit's sense of unjustified treatment suggests man's refusal to accept his fallen and sinful state; the climactic killing of the grandmother who offers forgiveness and love symbolizes the crucifixion and the refusal of grace. Both approaches have some validity, and I believe any complete interpretation of the story should recognize both of them. It does not seem adequate, however, merely to divide the story into different levels of meaning that occasionally overlap by sharing some details, to assume that The Misfit is in one sense a madman and in another sense a symbol of fallen man as though one were reading two different stories with some of the same characters and incidents. While such an attitude permits a greater complexity of response, it also destroys the wholeness of the story, and it opposes the Christian humanist's belief that existence is integral. It assumes that the psyche and the spirit are both important subjects and that one may do justice to both by considering them separately but equally.

From Kierkegaard's religious psychology, however, I have derived a third approach, not because increasing the number of levels will bring wholeness but because it will offer an integrated attitude in which the other two approaches will appear as complementary aspects of a whole. Kierkegaard describes two forms of the demonic man who wills to be himself in despair, the active and the passive forms, and both apply to The Misfit. He writes of the former:

> If the despairing *self* is *active*, it really is related to itself only as experimenting with whatsoever it be that it undertakes, however great it may be, however astonishing, however persistently carried out. It acknowledges no power over it, hence in the last resort it lacks seriousness and is able only to conjure up a show of seriousness when the self bestows upon its experiments its utmost attention. . . . The self is its own lord and master, so it is said, its own lord, and precisely this is despair, but so also is what it regards as its pleasure and enjoyment. However, by closer inspection one easily ascertains that this ruler is a king without a country, he rules really over nothing. (pp. 110–11)

The Misfit knows that he has to choose between God and himself as lord. He knows that Jesus threw everything off balance by raising the dead and that one must either "throw everything away and follow Him" or else deny salvation and "enjoy the few minutes you got left the best way you can" (*Good Man*, p. 28). His choice is based on two egoistic reasons. He claims that he was not there to know for sure that Jesus did what he said; thus, he precludes faith by making his own empirical knowledge a condition of acceptance. And he will not compromise his self-sufficiency:

> "If you would pray," the old lady said, "Jesus would help you."
> "That's right," The Misfit said.
> "Well then, why don't you pray?" she asked trembling with delight suddenly.
> "I don't want no hep," he said. "I'm doing all right by myself." (p. 26)

The Misfit, however, is not doing all right, for his actions are as futile as Kierkegaard's description claims. His actions are arbitrary in themselves, since they are merely experiments performed to demonstrate his independence and ability for self-assertion. They are important to him merely because he has committed them, because he bestows importance on them, and, since he is not omnipotent and thus meets retaliation, because he is punished for committing them. So he says, "I found out the crime don't matter. You can do one thing or you can do another, kill a man or take a tire off his car, because sooner or later you're going to forget what it was you done and just be punished for it" (pp. 26–27).

If we can accept the prison psychiatrist's records, The Misfit has already forgotten killing his father.[13] On this incident both the Freudian and allegorical approaches substantiate the existential reading. For the Freudian, intense anxiety develops from killing (or more usually the desire to kill) the father, since the father is loved and respected as well as hated. The amnesia which frees the Oedipal man from psychological suffering also frees the demonic man from the guilt that would refute his independence. If the demonic man is to be completely his own lord and master, he cannot admit an absolute outside of his own wishes; thus he cannot allow himself to feel guilty about what he has done, especially about the central act that has declared his independence from the father. Similarly, in terms of the Fall, man asserts himself against the power outside of himself; then he must forget the Fall to deny guilt and to deny that there was anything to fall from. Thus, both consciously through his statements on crimes and unconsciously through amnesia, The Misfit tries to deny the intrinsic importance of his actions, which have come to seem things alien from himself. As the active man who wills to be himself in despair, he lives in a shadow world of arbitrary gestures that are no more than expressions of his isolated self. At one point The Misfit does state one ultimate concern as the alternative to following Jesus: to enjoy oneself through meanness, because there is "no pleasure but meanness." But this sadistic hedonism is a hoax, for he does not enjoy killing. Unlike Bobby Lee, his chortling sidekick, The Misfit acts either disinterestedly or compulsively; and after he has killed the grandmother he admits, "It's no real pleasure in life" (p. 29). The usual interpretation of this statement is that The Misfit is passing judgment on his life, and this interpretation seems true, for the statement does have a terrifying effect, but it does not get far enough into the character. The Misfit is not only judging his life by the standard of pleasure, but he is also admitting implicitly that pleasure is not really the end of his actions. Hedonism is a comforting ethic for the sadist. It allows him to assert his independence from external responsibilities but also to explain his actions and to believe that they are founded on an ultimate concern that is comfortingly familiar and stable. But for The Misfit, as for other sadists, this simplified pleasure principle is only a rationalization. So, when he has compulsively killed the grandmother, not for pleasure but from fear and defensiveness, and when he has seen the yodeling Bobby Lee as caricaturing the pleasure of meanness, he admits that his professed motives are false. Since he acts solely in defiance and self-assertion, he has no appeal, not even to pleasure. As the man of defiant despair, the man who asserts his own absoluteness in solitude, The Misfit has complete freedom of choice insofar as no alternative is intrinsically better than any other, since there is no such thing as the good. When alternatives are equally meaningless, however, freedom of choice is useless. Thus, Kierkegaard claims that the defiant man is a king without a country. Even if The Misfit could escape completely what is pursuing him and what forces him to recoil from the grandmother, he would become only the lord of nothing, a condition suggested by his moments of terrifying detachment.

The Misfit is not only the active self that wills to be itself in despair, the defiant assertor of its own power and separateness; he also fits Kierkegaard's description of the passive form, which lives in spite rather than active defiance. The passive form is also a "despair of manliness," since the individual does will to be himself in disrelation to God, unlike the "womanly" despairers, Mrs. Cope or Mrs. McIntyre, who do not will to be themselves, who try desperately not to be themselves. The passive differs from the active form of the self in that it is concerned not with its power but with its suffering, its misery, its victimization; yet these two forms are complementary manifestations of the same egoism, as closely related as the paranoiac's feelings of grandeur and persecution. As Kierkegaard explains, the demonic sufferer will not accept help from without:

> He would rather rage against everything, he the one man in the whole of existence who is the most unjustly treated, to whom it is especially important to have his torment at hand, important that no one should take it from him—for thus he can convince himself that he is in the right. This at last becomes so firmly fixed in his head that for a very peculiar reason he is afraid of eternity—for the reason, namely, that it might rid him of his (demoniacally understood) infinite advantage over other men, his (demoniacally understood) justification for being what he is. (pp. 115–16)

Thus, while being offended by his suffering, he will not give up this claim against existence, this righteousness by reason of misery: "Revolting against the whole of existence, it thinks it has hold of a proof against it, against its goodness. This proof the despairer thinks he himself is" (p. 118).[14]

Similarly, The Misfit insists upon his justification through suffering and through unjust treatment. Speaking literally in reference to his imprisonment and criminal record, he claims that he now keeps a signed copy of everything he does so that he will be able to prove that he has not been treated right: "'I call myself The Misfit,' he said, 'because I can't make what all I done wrong fit what all I gone through in punishment'" (p. 28). The metaphorical implications of this claim extend far beyond legal matters: they suggest the disbeliever's claims against the goodness and justice of God. Shortly afterward, he explicitly makes the extension himself as he objects that he was not around to see whether Jesus raised the dead: "'It ain't right I wasn't there because if I had of been there I would of known . . . and I wouldn't be like I am now'" (p. 29). He complains that he suffers because of injustice and divine determination, but he will not accept divine help: "'I don't want no hep,' he said. 'I'm doing all right by myself'" (p. 26). Such contradictions are logically irreconcilable, but they are psychologically consistent in the absurd attitudes of the demonic man.

To approach The Misfit in such terms of the demonic is to find a means of reconciling the religious and psychological interpretations mentioned previously, for this approach maintains that the origins of such despair are in man's freely chosen disassociation from God but that the manifestations of the despair concern the clinical psychologist. The partial allegory of the Fall in the story is an anagogical rendering of The Misfit's rejection of God and his consequent estrangement. The clinical symptoms validate that estrangement through recognizable patterns of behavior. The Misfit is a complex but unified character; he is an enormous artistic achievement considering the economy with which he is developed in a few pages. One must be careful, however, not to develop the sentimental attachment against which Miss O'Connor once warned her audience (*Mystery and Manners*, p. 110). Esthetic value, as Kierkegaard knew, is not the same as ethical or religious value, and the capacity for grace is not the same as the acceptance of grace. In the end of the story it is not The Misfit, with his acute and interestingly perverted consciousness, who triumphs; it is the obtuse but good-hearted grandmother as she dies in a moment of intuitive selflessness. She performs the one act that The Misfit will not do, losing the self in order to gain it.

Miss O'Connor's estranged characters, in addition to being viewed primarily through Kierkegaard's concepts of the despair of womanliness and manliness, through the self's general relations to itself in despair, can also be considered in relation to a more familiar pair of complementary states, each of which is incomplete in itself. First, there are those characters who exalt intellectuality or common sense and deny their passions, their animality, and the power of the irrational. Then, there are those who exalt vitality and the Dionysian, who are superstitious in religion, and who try to control their lives through literal or metaphorical magic. Both kinds of characters are in despair, trying to escape anxiety and demonically treating the profane as the sacred, the part as the whole.

Joy-Hulga Hopewell of "Good Country People" is the most complex of Miss O'Connor's demonic intellectuals. A stout, thirty-two-year-old woman with a Ph.D. and a wooden leg, Hulga is in many ways a case study in repression and neurotic compensation, although she is not just that, as man is never just a psychological case to the Christian humanist. When she was ten years old, her leg was shot off in a hunting accident. At thirty-two she has never danced, never been kissed, and, in her mother's terms, has never had "any *normal* good times." Instead, she reads philosophy. Ironically, because of a bad heart (and perhaps because of her more psychological infirmities), Hulga lives at home on her mother's farm, surrounded by the unsophisticated and earthy people she scorns. Miss O'Connor emphasizes the sensuous and emotional sterility of the character by contrasting her with the daughters of the hired help: "Glynese, a redhead, was eighteen and had many admirers; Carramae, a blonde, was only fifteen but already married and pregnant" (*Good Man*, p. 170). Mrs. Freeman, the girls' mother, further intensifies the contrast by gossiping continuously and minutely about her daughters' bodily functions: she keeps the Hopewells informed daily about Carramae's morning sickness, with full accounts of her eating and vomiting, and she recounts how Glynese got rid of a sty by letting her chiropractic boyfriend pop her neck while she lay across the seat of his car. Thus, in the background of Hulga's life there is an intensely physical mixture of sexuality, courtship, and common bodily ailments: a continuous reminder that man is partly an animal.

Hulga, however, is intent on denying that such matters are important. Most obviously, she cultivates her ugliness, avoiding any social contests with the Glyneses of the world and opposing her mother's cheerful belief that "people who looked on the bright side of things would be beautiful even if they were not" (p. 175). She lumbers around the house in a sweatshirt with a faded cowboy on it, exaggerating her deformity and feeling continuous outrage. She is particularly proud of having changed her name from "Joy" to "Hulga": "One of her major triumphs was that her mother had not been able to turn her dust into Joy, but the greater one was that she had been able to turn it herself into Hulga" (p. 174). Obviously, Hulga has not succeeded in becoming indifferent to her deformity; she is preoccupied with it, intent upon proving an indifference, which is disproved by the intent. Because she cannot really admit to herself that she is infirm, that she is dust, she tries to remake herself into something more apparently ludicrous than dust, into Hulga; thereby, she will seem to be in control of her condition, to have willed herself to be deformed as a jesting reply to the

"normal" people around her. Like The Misfit, she even trea-
sures her deformity and suffering for making her different,
and she is quite sensitive about her wooden leg and her
adopted name, for they are very personal matters and are
important to her as psychological symbols. In fact, she fan-
cifully, yet really quite seriously, attributes special powers to
her new name and the self-willed ugliness it represents: "She
had a vision of the name working like the ugly sweating
Vulcan who stayed in the furnace and to whom, presumably,
the goddess had to come when called" (p. 174). Through
this brief fantasy, with its clear sexual implications, the ugly
outcast triumphs, as in the common mythical pattern of the
dwarfs, humpbacks, and ugly magicians of the world who
enchant the beautiful princesses. But what magic could
come from dust, from an ordinary crippled girl who looked
on the bright side of things? Better to be a sweating Vulcan,
especially if one could feel responsible for the transformation
and if one still knew that beneath the disguise was another
self, laughing at the masquerade.

To supplement her mortification of the flesh, Hulga
also maintains a feeling of intellectual superiority by con-
founding wit with wisdom. Because she realizes that the
people around her are often foolishly conventional in their
ideas and values, she thinks that she lives without illusions,
which is ridiculous, because her illusions are only more
sophisticated than theirs. In a parody of popularized existentialism, she claims that she is "one of those people who see
through to nothing" and that she has "a kind of salvation"
because she sees that there is nothing to see (p. 191). In
both of these claims she is proudly asserting her role as the
mocker and negater, but in neither does she understand
that "nothing" can be the object of experience. Her claim
that there is "nothing to see" means merely that she does
not find anything to see, not that "nothing" can be the
object of metaphorical sight. Her "nothing" is hypothetical,
abstract, a philosophical cliché; it has little in common with

the "nothing" that Kierkegaard and other existentialists make the object of dread. This is made clear by the passage which Mrs. Hopewell finds in one of the books Hulga has been reading:

> "Science, on the other hand, has to assert its soberness and seriousness afresh and declare that it is concerned solely with what-is. Nothing—how can it be for science anything but a horror and a phantasm? If science is right, then one thing stands firm: science wishes to know nothing of nothing. Such is after all the strictly scientific approach to Nothing. We know it by wishing to know nothing of Nothing." These words had been underlined with a blue pencil and they worked on Mrs. Hopewell like some evil incantation in gibberish. She shut the book quickly and went out of the room as if she were having a chill. (pp. 176–77)

Although Mrs. Hopewell's superstitious response to the unknown is comic, it is intuitively right. For Hulga such a passage *is* an incantation to ward off the experience of nothing, and Hulga remains emotionally safe because she, too, wishes to know nothing of nothing. Thus, whatever is disturbing she eliminates through a trite nihilism, which she in turn renders harmless to herself through a scientific positivism (which, if the argument were extended, would be negated by the nihilism). Her philosophical position is nonsensical, for it has developed out of neurotic needs, her need to escape her socially and physically incomplete self, her dread of nothing, her realization that she is dust like all of mankind. So she becomes a ridiculous case of the satirist satirized and the rationalist revealed as irrational.

She is as fully absurd when she sets out to enlighten an apparently naive and religious Bible salesman, an action which she thinks to be altruistic and objectively experimental. Her motives are actually selfish and psychologically complex. She clearly wants to disillusion the young man to demonstrate her superiority, to recreate him as she thinks she has recreated herself, and she wants to continue her defensive attack on the good country people whom she scorns. Yet her plan for his philosophical education reveals less obvious, perhaps even more repressed, motives. She intends to seduce him and then lead him into the realization that there is nothing to see: "She imagined that she took his remorse in hand and changed it into a deeper understanding of life. She took all his shame away and turned it into something useful" (p. 186). Miss O'Connor's choice of seduction as Hulga's method is good comic psychology. Hulga's assumption that sexual remorse and shame would lead to her pseudo-nihilistic view of life reveals much about her own unconscious and the sexually neurotic bases of her philosophy. Also, one might well suspect the disinterestedness of a plan that would involve her own sexual initiation, especially since it would be executed on an apparent bumpkin who would offer little psychological threat to the inexperienced woman and tutor.

The murkiness of Hulga's motives and her lack of self-knowledge make her quite vulnerable to the bogus rube; in fact, she even considers running away with him. In the first place, she is moved that the boy sees "the truth about her," since he claims that her wooden leg makes her different from everyone else. She does not realize that he is even more of a morbid fetishist than she is. She imagines that, after they have run away, "every night he would take the leg off and every morning put it back on again" (p. 193), a fantasy that suggests her neurotically sublimated sexuality, her desire to relax her defenses, and her need to admit dependence. In the second place, she sentimentally has imagined the boy as a natural man: good, innocent, childlike, and intuitive, the antithesis of what she thinks herself to be. This image, which he helps to encourage, is an obverse reflex of her cynicism; it is almost proverbial that the same person may well be a worldly cynic and a naive sentimentalist, since he who is not whole may see alternately from different extremes.

The climax of the story is a violent attack on Hulga's illusions. As the Bible salesman drops his disguise as good country people, he reveals that he is more cynical than she, that his sexual attitudes toward her are brutal and obscene, and, most importantly, that his belief in nothing is far more radical than hers. Faced with what seemed to be an adoring, childlike boy, Hulga felt safe enough to experience emotions that she had previously protected herself against; when her defenses have been lessened, she is confronted with an image of what she has pretended to be, with a real, diabolical nihilist who exposes her name-changing and philosophizing as mere adolescent posturing. Having been emotionally and psychologically seduced, Hulga is the one who is educated; for the first time she is forced to "see *through* to nothing," an experience far less comfortable than she had imagined. As she is left behind in a state of near shock, without her glasses, her wooden leg, or her feigned self-sufficiency, her old self has been burned away, and she might be forced into a free choice that may be a new beginning. Perhaps it might even lead to her accepting her own body with its deformity and sexual desire, to accepting the ironies inherent in man's spiritual-corporeal nature.

Asbury Fox in "The Enduring Chill' is quite similar to Hulga in character, situation, and defensive illusion. Asbury is no philosopher, but he has an "artistic temperament," which keeps him disdainfully aloof from the dairy farm on which he has grown up. Again, the consciously intellectual character is surrounded by an earthy life he finds disgusting and a bit humiliating. Instead of Glynese and Carramae there are dairy cows, but the effect is much the same. In fact, Mrs. Fox's conversation about her cows recalls Mrs. Freeman's about her daughters: "This was largely about cows with names like Daisy and Bessie Button and their intimate functions—their mastitis and their screwworms and their abortions" (*Everything*, p. 95). When Asbury arrived home from New York, he became immediately aware again that this humiliating earthiness was imposing on him; as he rode up the driveway, he saw that "a small, walleyed Guernsey was watching him steadily as if she sensed some bond between them" (p. 88). But Asbury will admit no bonds with the cows; his vain intellect will not be compromised by his animality. Nevertheless, he will not accept the affected oriental mysticism of his New York friend Goetz, since it would deny his significance as an individual. Denying his relation both to the cows below and the spirit above, he tries to work out his private substitute for salvation.

He has failed completely as a writer, and he seems to be dying at twenty-five from a strange prolonged illness. But he has made adequate psychological provisions for his failure, and he is intent on keeping it from destroying his vanity. Most obviously he has the pride of introspection; admitting to himself that he has no talent despite his desire to create, he can feel, like Hulga, that he has no illusions. If he has not seen through to nothing, he has at least seen through himself, and he has written a long letter ("such a letter as Kafka had addressed to his father" [p. 91]) to introduce his mother to reality. But real self-knowledge would not be an adequate defense for Asbury. His is only a partial insight combined with sufficient escapes and twisted into a comic self-justification. For one thing, he has convinced himself that his mother has caused his failure, that her solicitude and dullness have stifled his imagination. Although this claim probably has some truth in it, especially since he has become self-consciously esthetic in rebellion against her, it hardly justifies his role as a victim. Still more importantly, he cherishes the image of himself as tragic hero, not just because it shifts the blame and demands pity, but also because it enables him to succeed as a dramatic character where he had failed as an author. Art has given him the chance to be redeemed by living his one great work, and in the "unique tragedy of his death," he finds great meaning. He sees himself as dying of a broken imagination because his spirit is too great to endure the failure forced upon it: "Death was coming to him legitimately, as a justification, as a gift from life. That was his greatest triumph" (p. 99).

Asbury, however, is as much an artistic and spiritual failure in creating his own tragedy as he was in writing his lifeless works. His "unique tragedy" is a trite, third-rate decadent melodramatic prose-poem. It has stock characters, like the *fin de siècle* Jesuit whose face shows a "subtle blend of asceticism and corruption." It has some sensuous morbidity, a good deal of dated nonsense about serving the god, Art, and very little action. Asbury even intends to conclude his life with a "meaningful experience," a sophisticated talk with a priest about Joyce or a smoke with the Negro dairy workers. But he cannot even bring off this artificial tragedy, since reality keeps intruding on his artifice. The Jesuit who comes to his sickbed turns out to be a half-blind, half-deaf, old Irishman who knows nothing about Joyce, who insists on discussing Asbury's neglect of prayers and the catechism, and who calls him a "lazy ignorant conceited youth." The Negroes are painfully ill at ease, and in their cultivatedly polite and cheerful manner they assure him that he looks fine. Worst of all, old Dr. Block, whom Asbury has scorned, finds out that he is not going to die after all, that he has undulant fever ("same as Bang's in a cow") from drinking unpasteurized milk. After these attacks on his fantasies, Asbury is left to endure his chronic illness and to experience the terrifying grace of God, which descends metaphorically as the bird image stained on his bedroom ceiling.

This story, like "Revelation," has been criticized for ending with a religious vision that has not been prepared for, but again the criticism seems to neglect the extent to which religious concerns are interfused throughout. The final symbol of the Holy Ghost is anticipated in cleverly contrasted images of birds. For example, Asbury wanted to let his imagination free like a hawk and "set it 'whirling off into the widening gyre' (Yeats)" (p. 91); this misquoted line from Yeats is doubly ironic, because it is ridiculously pretentious and because in "The Second Coming" it refers to anarchy when "the centre cannot hold" and the "falcon cannot hear the falconer." In the story it becomes a comment on the futility of seeking creativity and freedom in complete independence from man's center. Also, with perhaps too much preciousness, Miss O'Connor has named the New York Jesuit whom Asbury meets "Ignatius V*ogle*, S. J." Finally and most obviously, Asbury has used the bird-shaped stain since childhood as a symbol of what he fears; so, the religious connotations, prepared by both Jesuits' emphasis on the Holy Ghost, accrue about the psychological symbol.

Still more importantly, Asbury is well prepared for his revelation. Like Hulga, he is forced to experience what he has pretended to believe; despair, which has been partly an affectation, becomes real and not very romantically appealing; and as his defenses collapse, his fears, desires, and past experiences coalesce in the final vision. The story is so thoroughly structured that a psychologist could probably account for the vision in purely natural terms. Miss O'Connor has different beliefs, although they extend rather than ignore the psychologist's: grace can be experienced by any man when he is fleeing from it, especially when he stumbles in his flight. In Hulga and Asbury, she represents such flight as the domestication of despair, either through philosophical or artistic posturing. Although the specific forms of these two characters' estrangement are fairly modern—popularized existentialism and late romantic estheticism—the basic patterns are not; self-congratulating nihilists and melancholics are common enough to have provided stock characters for every period of English and American literature. But no matter how much the intellectual deifies himself, there is always a cow with Bang's ready to prove kinship.

Mrs. May of "Greenleaf" also has much trouble with cattle, and she betrays some of the same fears of the flesh. Mrs. May is hardly an intellectual. In fact, in her concern for decency, hard work, and social position, she is quite similar to the philistine women discussed earlier. However, she is a farm owner only by necessity, since she had to move to the country when her husband died, leaving just the farm which he had bought as a real estate investment. Being industrious and self-possessed, she has made the best of her lot, struggling to keep the place intact for her ungrateful sons; but her managing seems more like running a business than working a farm. Far from taking Mrs. Hopewell's interest in the bodily functions of her cows, Mrs. May tries to maintain gentility and an efficient aloofness. In doing so, she reveals a basic spiritual inadequacy that (as with Hulga and Asbury) is inseparable from her compulsive disdain for the body.

Her sexual repressions are revealed mostly through her relations with the runaway scrub bull that has invaded her farm and that threatens to ruin her herd. The bull is presented repeatedly as an irrepressible sexual force: he "likes to bust loose" from the pens in which he is put; he smashes into a pickup truck; and, as he grazes under Mrs. May's window at night, he seems like an "uncouth country suitor" or a "patient god" that has come to woo her (*Everything*, pp. 39, 38, 25, 24). Moreover, the bull belongs to O. T. and E. T. Greenleaf, the hired man's sons, whom Mrs. May considers "scrub human" trash but who, nevertheless, continue to thrive and grow richer while she struggles to stay genteel. The Greenleaf boys, who resemble Faulkner's second and third generation Snopeses, are long-legged, raw-boned, red-skinned farmers with "bright grasping fox-colored eyes." They are virile, shrewd, and coarse, the suitable owners of the intruding bull. In contrast, Mrs. May's sons suggest the end of a thinning family stock. Scofield, unmarried at thirty-six, has a broad, pleasant, smiling face and sells "nigger-insurance" because there is more money in it than in any other kind. Wesley, who had rheumatic fever at seven and must eat a salt-free diet, is a bitter "intellectual," who teaches at a nearby college he scorns and talks about traveling but, like most of Miss O'Connor's inert intellectuals, never leaves home. Neither of the boys will have anything to do with cows, let alone the scrub bull. Mrs. May, however, must finally confront this Dionysian "sport." As she drives into the fields with Mr. Greenleaf so that he can kill the bull, she feels exhilarated, in part because he is doing what she wants, because she is going to get even with the Greenleafs, and because she will get rid of a main symbol of her troubles, but also because, as she exclaims, "spring is here," a springtime that, reinforced by the names "May" and "Greenleaf," suggests a reawakening fertility. The story reaches it climax as she is gored by the bull, who gallops out of the dark woods with a "gay almost rocking gait" and then buries his head in her lap, "like a wild tormented lover." Despite her attempts to suppress whatever she finds coarse in nature, she cannot will out of existence this uncouth suitor who must be heeded and who triumphs in erotic killing.

There is also much in the story to indicate that the bull is symbolically divine as well as libidinous, a force from above as well as from within. Outside her window he is likened to a "patient god"; his horns seem wreathed by bits of torn hedge; and he is several times associated with the sun, once clearly suggesting a divine manifestation ("she saw a darker shape that might have been [the sun's] shadow cast at an angle, moving among them" [pp. 37–38]). Above all, the ending implies unmistakably a religious revelation; after she was gored, "she continued to stare straight ahead but the entire scene in front of her had changed—the tree line was a dark wound in a world that was nothing but sky—and she had the look of a person whose sight has been suddenly restored but who finds the light unbearable" (p. 52). The images of a wound, the sky, sight, and light show clearly a concern beyond Freudianism. One commentator goes so far as to claim that "the bull, then, symbolizes the justice of God in its destructiveness and the love of Christ in its function of saving Mrs. May by revealing the truth to her," [15] an interpretation that is certainly valid but incomplete, since (except for an analogy with Zeus and Europa) it has nothing to say of the persistent sexual theme.

As in the case of The Misfit, there is the danger of breaking the story into different levels, thus producing a case history of sexual repression or an account of religious enlightenment or a clever juggling of both. But the story is unified and does not merely offer something for everyone regardless of where he finds his pleasure. For one thing, Mrs. May's religious and sexual attitudes are frequently associated. The narrator explains that "she thought the word, Jesus, should be kept inside the church building like other words inside the bedroom" (p. 31). Jesus and sexuality are permissible only under tight limits of decorum, because Mrs. May does not believe seriously in either but is disturbed by both. Shame of the spirit and shame of the body are here two similar consequences of her bourgeois gentility. Later she says to her sons, "I don't like to hear you boys make jokes about religion. . . . If you would go to church, you would meet some nice girls" (p. 35). Here she not only associates religion and sexuality, but she shows that she has almost managed to reduce both of them to harmlessly useful social concerns; meeting nice girls in church—nominal Christianity and nominal sexuality. Behind Mrs. May's prattle is the terrible fact that her view of existence has been forcibly narrowed to a safe, civilized mediocrity that cannot accommodate impulses from spirit or id; and in denying man's kinship with animals and with God, she is intent upon making him into a predictable and dull machine. (In fact, while she scorns the Greenleafs' religion and virility, she envies O. T. and E. T. for their farm machinery, particularly their milking machines.)

With such associations established, the use of the bull as the main symbol becomes complex, not just manifold, but truly complex. Very likely the Bull-God is intended to suggest Zeus and, by extension, a manifestation of God; perhaps in this respect he even connotes Christ as the bridegroom and the wreathed sacrificial victim, although the connections here become tenuous. Yet, in what must be ironic contrast to these symbolic meanings, the bull also suggests the object of Dionysian worship, which would mean that Mrs. May would have Pasiphaë as well as Europa in her symbolic lineage. The worship of the Bull-God in Dionysian rites hardly involves Christian agape. Instead, there is the exalted and frenzied attempt to become one with the god, to destroy the self entirely through ecstasy. D'Arcy discusses in some detail this self-sacrificial extreme of love, and he finds it a religiously and psychologically distorted attitude toward the deity, although a partial component in full Christian love and a valuable disturbance to the secular humanist's ideal of poise and moderation.[16]

Perhaps these complex relationships can be most clearly interpreted in terms of reaction. Since Mrs. May has so rigidly repressed her sexual and animal being, she experiences sexuality as erotic destruction; since she has so intently ignored God, she is racked by an unendurable light of revelation and by a purifying love that must destroy the old self. The violent experience is necessary to help break the defenses, but it is not therefore to be seen as an ideal state in itself. Because she has been so partial and extreme, her awakening comes through opposite extremes, which are also partial. She even experiences revelation through a demonic form: she becomes aware of God through a symbolic, Dionysian immolation of her self, which is not to say that such immolation is a Christian ideal any more than being pierced by a bull is an ideal form of sexual behavior. Such patterns of reaction also help to explain why Miss O'Connor so often uses satanic instruments to enlighten her characters: she is not only showing that God moves in mysterious ways and brings good out of evil; she is also exploring the psychological and religious view that demonic characters experience God's mercy through demonic structures that oppose or caricature their own forms of idolatry.

At the opposite extreme from these rationalistic and repressed characters, Miss O'Connor has created some demonic characters who are dedicatedly irrational, even Diony-sian and superstitiously ritualistic. The Tarwaters of *The Violent Bear It Away* have strong traces of these qualities, which necessarily complicate the reader's responses to their religion. In Miss O'Connor's short stories such characters usually serve as foils to the main characters or demonic instru-ments of revelation (like the satanic boys in "A Circle in the Fire" and "The Lame Shall Enter First"). When they do appear as main characters, they are unwittingly Dionysian, worshiping strange dark gods they do not recognize.

Mrs. Greenleaf does not even appear in the story, "Green-leaf," but a few brief accounts of her actions establish her as a central antithesis to Mrs. May. The hired man's wife is a superstitious prayer healer; she cuts morbid stories out of the newspapers, buries them in the woods, and prays, rolls, and groans over them for an hour or so. Her yard looks like a dump, and her five daughters are filthy and dip snuff. Mrs. Greenleaf is definitely trash. Moreover, her prayer healing is clearly associated with sexual drives, which further under-scores the association of religion and sexuality in Mrs. May. (Mrs. May's feeling that "the word, Jesus, should be kept in-side the church building like other words inside the bedroom" is specifically called forth when she hears the healer scream-ing "Jesus" during one of her sessions.) One of her healings in the woods symbolically and psychologically unites the main themes of the story: " 'Oh Jesus, stab me in the heart!' Mrs. Greenleaf shrieked. 'Jesus, stab me in the heart!' and she fell back flat in the dirt, a huge human mound, her legs and arms spread out as if she were trying to wrap them around the earth" (p. 31). The religious frenzy, the sexual images, the attempt to merge with the object of worship, the longing for death—all are fused in an orgiastic rite, anticipating the final scene in which the bull literally stabs Mrs. May in the heart.

While Mrs. Greenleaf is spiritually more vital than Mrs. May, the former's faith is still corrupted by the demonic qualities that make it grotesque. Kierkegaard claims that "superstition and unbelief are both of them forms of unfreedom. In superstition there is conceded to objectivity a power like that of Medusa's head to turn subjectivity to stone, and unfreedom does not will to have the spell broken." [17] Despite his fervor, the superstitious man lacks certitude. In his human anxiety he cannot be satisfied with faith alone; thus, he becomes a magician performing the initiate's gestures to prove, appease, and even coerce God. Unlike the unbeliever, he has a strong sense of mystery, but he also believes that he can control the mysterious. Whereas Mrs. Cope avoids thinking about calamities and Mrs. Pritchard avidly gossips about them, Mrs. Greenleaf sets about to rectify them by prayer healing. Like the other two women, she, too, is trying to escape the unknown that has produced the raped women, burned children, and divorced movie stars she prays for.

Although within the story itself this judgment of Mrs. Greenleaf can be divined only from the comic treatment and the parallels to Mrs. May's death, Miss O'Connor is quite explicit about superstition in "The River." The Reverend Bevel Summers, who preaches at the river gathering, insists repeatedly that *he* cannot heal the sick and the immersions in the muddy water will not heal them: " 'If you just come to see can you leave your pain in the river, you ain't come for Jesus. You can't leave your pain in the river,' he said. 'I never told nobody that' " (*Good Man*, p. 40). Nevertheless, some of the believers insist that he is a healer, and one of them grotesquely caricatures their superstitious attitudes:

> While he was talking a fluttering figure had begun to move forward with a kind of butterfly movement—an old woman with flapping arms whose head wobbled as if it might fall off any second. She managed to lower herself at the edge of the bank and let her arms churn in the water. Then she bent farther and pushed her face down in it and raised herself up finally, streaming wet; and still flapping, she turned a time or two in a blind circle until someone reached out and pulled her back into the group. (p. 42)

The preacher still maintains that the water will not heal them, that "there ain't but one river and that's the River of Life, made out of Jesus's blood," and that only in that River of pain can they be saved. Yet many of the people cannot accept these unaided demands of faith and need a miracle worker to sustain them. Thus, they have something in common with Mr. Paradise, the old unbeliever who mocks Summers for not curing cancer.

The distinction between superstition and faith helps to clarify the ending of the story in which the four- or five-year-old child, who is practically ignored by his parents, drowns himself trying to find the Kingdom of Christ in the river. Insofar as he has been baptized and has finally found a home and his Father, his drowning is a real spiritual passage. Certainly this is intended to be the most important significance of the violent scene, for as Miss O'Connor has said (probably about *The Violent Bear It Away* but with relevance to this story), "If I write a novel in which the central action is a baptism, I know that for the larger percentage of my readers, baptism is a meaningless rite; therefore, I have to imbue this action with an awe and terror which will suggest its awful mystery." [18] But at the same time the child drowns himself because, in his loneliness and longing, he cannot differentiate between the River of Life and the literal river, between faith and superstition. In seeking Christ under the water, he resembles those people who wish to lay their pain in the muddy river, because they, too, are lonely and anxious.

In a final extension of the subject, one could say that all of the demonic characters are superstitious and irrational, no matter how much they pride themselves in their rationality. Since the "demonic" in Tillich's sense, which I have been using throughout, means a worship of what is not God, hence a worship of idols and demons, such characters are serving dark forces even though they do not know it. Appropriately such unwitting devil worshipers have superstitious charms and rituals by which they try to appease the religious and psychological demons that possess them. Mrs. Cope obsessively pulls up the weeds and nut grass, Mrs. Turpin recites to herself the hierarchy of social classes, Hulga Hopewell underlines in blue pencil the incantation in gibberish that claims science will know nothing of nothing.

Mr. Fortune in "A View of the Woods" illustrates well the idolatry, evil, and destructiveness of the demonic, even when its professed object is civilization. Although he is an old country man, Fortune believes in progress, in a paved road with a grocery store and gas station in front of his farm house and in the town of Fortune, Georgia, which he imagines will someday be built on the land he is selling off to developers. He also believes in his nine-year-old granddaughter, Mary Fortune Pitts, the only one of his daughter's children who looks like him and not like Pitts, the son-in-law whom the old man detests. He has secretly willed his land to the child, and he does what he can to make her side with him against the rest of the family.

Although Fortune is irascible and seemingly independent, there are indications that he is not as secure as he would like to think. He is seventy-nine years old, and, as the narrator says, "anyone over sixty years of age is in an uneasy position unless he controls the greater interest and every now and then he gave the Pittses a practical lesson by selling off a lot" (*Everything*, p. 56). He will not admit that his duty-proud daughter does take care of him, and he is furiously jealous of Mary Fortune Pitts's ties to her father. One begins to see that Fortune's attitudes toward progress and his granddaughter are not only humorous, but also demonic. For one thing, he uses both to attack his daughter and son-in-law because they are replacing him, because he is becoming practically irrelevant apart from his land holdings, his relations with the child, and his belief that he is more up-to-date than they are. For another thing, he uses them unconsciously to deny his inevitable end. Through his belief in progress, and thus his vicarious participation in the future, and through his identification with the child who looks and acts like him, he can feel as though he will live indefinitely. Miss O'Connor is thereby parodying two of the most pervasive American dreams of an artificial eternity, wherein the future, either of mankind or the family, is substituted for the eternal.

The specifically demonic nature of such attitudes is shown symbolically. Miss O'Connor describes the man to whom Fortune sells his front lot for a gas station, a man named Tilman who buys and sells almost anything, as satanically serpentine: "He sat habitually with his arms folded on the counter and his insignificant head weaving snake-fashion above them. He had a triangular-shaped face with the point at the bottom and the top of his skull was covered with a cap of freckles. His eyes were green and very narrow and his tongue was always exposed in his partly opened mouth" (p. 76). Also, the symbolic object of Fortune's worship of progress, a steam shovel that is digging up his cow pasture to build a fishing club, is described as a "yellow monster"; the old man and the child sit for hours "watching the big disembodied gullet gorge itself on the clay, then, with the sound of a deep sustained nausea and a slow mechanical revulsion, turn and spit it up" (p. 55).

Dealing with the commercial devil and worshiping a mechanical monster finally ends disastrously. Furious at the child when she sides with her father against selling the front lot that permits a view of the symbolic woods, Fortune decides to whip her as Pitts has often done. They fight, the girl gets him down, and he looks into his own image, telling him that he has been whipped by pure Pitts. In a frantic reaction against "the face that was his own but had dared to call itself Pitts," he hits her head against a rock until he kills her. As he dies of a heart attack, he imagines himself drowning in the manmade lake where there is no one to help him, only the yellow monster, eating clay. The immediate cause of his killing the child is his inability to admit that there could be any "Pitts" in himself, in a Fortune who knows what is what. In this he resembles Asbury Fox, who cannot admit his kinship with cows, and Mrs. Turpin, who does her best to deny her kinship with white trash and hogs. This motive for the killing is theoretically precise, for underlying the demonic destructiveness is pride, the pride that enables man to reject God and to establish idols. And underlying pride is dread, a basic condition of man that can be adequately overcome only by faith. But if one will not have faith and will not accept grace, Miss O'Connor believes, one becomes estranged and demonic—the philistine, trying to imprison the possible in the probable; the anti-Christ, asserting himself in defiance or in self-pitying spite; the rationalist, refusing to admit his animal nature; the superstitious man, defying reason in order to manipulate life magically. The consequences of such action are of this world as well as the next, Miss O'Connor repeatedly suggests, because man's spiritual nature is inseparable from other aspects of his being, and the man in rebellion against God is also in rebellion against himself.

3. Exorcism and Grace

$\mathcal{T}he$ demonic in Miss O'Connor's stories includes not only the dread from which her characters try to escape, but another complementary cause: endless desire or concupiscence. Unlike dread, concupiscence shows in an obvious way man's incompleteness and his desire to be fulfilled by something outside of himself. For the Christian humanist this desire is basically an unrecognized longing for God, for restoration through grace. A good beginning point in considering Miss O'Connor's representation of the whole man and restorative grace is a last form of the demonic, the misdirected hunger that implies grace as its final object.

Concupiscence does not refer to all earthly desire, or rather it would do so only for the Manichae who scorned all physical existence, an attitude that certainly does not apply to Miss O'Connor's work. It refers to an excessive desire for things of this world, not only for sexual pleasures, to which it is sometimes limited, but for anything finite, including knowledge and honor. Since concupiscence treats a finite object of desire as though it were infinite, it is a form of the demonic, which worships the finite. Like dread, it be-

71

gins in man's spiritual-corporeal nature and in his longing to
escape from incompleteness and possibility, and, like dread,
it grows with his estrangement from God. Like dread, too, it
ultimately has no finite object; as "nothing" is the real object
of dread, so it is the real object of endless desire. Thus, the
man who either dreads or desires "nothing" can be healed
only from beyond a world of things. Since his dread and his
longing are infinite, they require infinite help. But when finite
man cannot have sufficient faith, he turns for help to the
finite world. Man tries to reduce his infinite dread to fears
of specific objects he can understand and perhaps control; the
substitution is a sham, a creation of phobias that bind him
and eventually fail to distract him. Similarly, he tries to fix his
infinite longings to definite objects and becomes neurotically
obsessed with things that can never fully satisfy him.

The concupiscent man may be the compulsive miser
or glutton or lecher, who acts as though a limitless quantity of
his fixated pleasure would finally quiet his appetite. Or he
may be the Faustian romantic whose objects are limitless
because undefinable, who finds no object adequate but will
not abandon his quest for finite perfection. He may be the
man driven by a Freudian wish for death and nirvana to
still the endless, frustrated libido that desires more pleasure
than reality can provide. In all of these cases, the religious
psychologist finds different manifestations of the same general condition, estrangement from God. Paul Tillich, for
example, claims that Freud's pessimism comes inevitably
from the failure to realize that "endless libido" is not characteristic of man's essential nature, that it is a "mark of man's
estrangement." [1] Consequently, the theologian does not end
in romantic melancholy or psychological pessimism; considering concupiscence a symptom of spiritual disrelation rather
than an essential state of man, he finds the cure outside the
naturalist's dead end.

If concupiscence signifies man's estrangement from God
and from his essential self, however, it also signifies his

divinity. Man cannot be satisfied, for he will have no less than all. As Carlyle wrote in *Sartor Resartus*:

Man's Unhappiness, as I construe, comes of his Greatness; it is because there is an Infinite in him, which with all his cunning he cannot quite bury under the Finite. Will the whole Finance Ministers and Upholsterers and Confectioners of modern Europe undertake, in joint-stock company, to make one Shoeblack HAPPY? They cannot accomplish it, above an hour or two; for the Shoeblack also has a Soul quite other than his Stomach; and would require, if you consider it, for his permanent satisfaction and saturation, simply this allotment, no more, and no less: God's *infinite Universe altogether to himself*, therein to enjoy infinitely, and to fill every wish as fast as it rose. (chap. 9, "The Everlasting Yea")

As Carlyle's tone indicates, and as I think Miss O'Connor would have agreed, this universal appetite is to be condemned as egoism and ignorance of one's true ends; nevertheless, it still testifies that man is a spiritual as well as corporeal creature, that he has a soul which cannot be filled through the stomach no matter how fast he eats. Correspondingly, Miss O'Connor sometimes uses man's restlessness and desires, as she uses his anxiety, to show that he has not completely lost his essential self or his possibilities for salvation.

One commentator has objected that Miss O'Connor "seemed to find in man a drive to believe in Christ as universal as the hunger or sex drive" and that her use of an allegorical Everyman as hero of each novel shows a tenuous assumption that man is innately religious.[2] This description seems quite valid, but I do not agree that it should be an objection to her work. Miss O'Connor joins many excellent philosophers and theologians in assuming that man is a spiritual creature and that human problems cannot be adequately considered without regard to his full being. Her assumption is not merely a personal or sectarian aberration too peculiar to serve as a premise for fiction; it is quite as tenable, I think, as the Freudian or Jungian assumptions that have served, intentionally or not, as the beliefs behind much twentieth-century literature. Any author who is concerned with man rather than just with individuals will have to have some basic assumptions, no matter how unobtrusive, about man's essential nature. If he assumes that man's essential motivations are only the demonstrable hunger and sex drives, he will not only write a dull and narrow book, he will also work from a belief far less tenable than Miss O'Connor's. Perhaps the criticism comes from a misunderstanding of what Miss O'Connor's allegorical method implies. Clearly, she did not believe that everyone has an overt and recognized drive to believe in Christ. Her stories make that quite clear in the many minor characters who do not become conscious of any religious drives, even though they show demonic symptoms. The main characters *are* the protagonists, in effect, because they do experience the self-revelations which are possible for all men although not accepted by all; "Everyman" represents what is essential in mankind, but, as Miss O'Connor demonstrates, men may work intently to deny or sublimate that essence. A statistical report on the number of people who recognize in themselves a drive to believe in God will not settle the problem of man's essential nature, any more than such a report will prove whether or not all men have Oedipal desires and share in the collective unconscious. Only an extreme empiricist could believe that ultimate philosophical questions can be solved through demonstration.

Although the main characters of her novels struggle openly with their drives to believe in Christ, the religious drive in Miss O'Connor's short stories is initially as sublimated as the religious dread. Many of her characters discussed previously could be analyzed in terms of concupiscence as well as dread, but I shall open some new territory by considering another more pointed case, O. E. Parker of "Parker's Back." Obadiah Elihu Parker is probably Miss O'Connor's most obvious case of sublimated will to believe. In fact, the story suffers from being too pat, too explicit throughout in its symbols and authorial comments. The better stories move from an apparently naturalistic surface into an increasing sense of deeper concerns. They expand the reader's vision, often suddenly, so that early details take on new meaning as new patterns emerge. "Parker's Back," however, insists too much and too often on its central themes. In doing so the story is symbolically precise, but it does not thoroughly embody its religious mysteries in manners, and the reader may well feel a bit too carefully managed, as though the mysteries were not very mysterious after all. But these literary weaknesses make the story a convenient one for studying the theme of concupiscence and what it masks.

Parker is obsessed with the desire to be tattooed. Until he saw a tattooed man at a fair when he was fourteen, he had never felt wonder or thought that "there was anything out of the ordinary about the fact that he existed" (*Everything*, p. 223). However, with that exotic and superstitious experience, he vaguely became aware of a capacity to respond and desire. Although not strictly religious, the experience was a movement of the spirit; it was one of the "gracious" moments that seem to be given and which other cultures have attributed to muses or ghosts. So he begins to be tattooed, starts getting into fights (the awakening spirit is not always as well-mannered as the sleeping one), joins the navy (partly in fear of his mother's Baptist religion), and almost succeeds in blending into the mechanical ship ("except for his eyes, which were the same pale slate-color as the ocean and reflected the immense spaces around him as if they were a microcosm of the mysterious sea" [p. 224]). He continues to be tattooed, choosing figures that are more animated, but he becomes increasingly dissatisfied, a feeling that, in Carlyle's terms, "comes of his greatness." For one thing, the overall effect of the tattoos is haphazard and botched, because it does not come from a unifying center; it comes from random, compulsive, and unexamined attempts to quiet his vague longings. For another, each tattoo gives him satisfaction only until the novelty wears off, and O. E. is running out of skin.

Most importantly, the tattoos cannot fulfill the undefined demands of his spirit, since they are only substitutes for the spiritual consummation he desires. His tattoos are a form of idolatry, but that makes them a form of worship and a sign of the spirit, however misdirected and frustrating. The panther, lion, serpents, eagles, and hawks that inhabit his skin and seem to rage inside him in his dissatisfaction are symbols of his demonic possession, but they also have an oblique relation to the apocalyptic animals of the prophet, which they parody. To feel such despair is a great suffering, but never to have felt it is a greater misfortune.

Parker's religious drives are also betrayed through his attitudes toward the woman he marries. He does not know why he courts this ugly, poor farm girl, and he develops a nervous tic wondering why he stays with her after they are married and she has become pregnant. Sarah Ruth is a skinny, nasty, self-righteous daughter of a fundamentalist preacher, and she scorns his tattoos as vanity. But he cannot run away from her absoluteness, her judgments, her demands upon him. Although she, too, is somewhat demonic in the arrogance and animosity of her Manichean religion, she suggests something that he needs and has not been able to achieve through his botched assortment of tattoos. Since she has little meat on her, he can feel her muscles and bones (unlike the "hefty young blonde" he fabricates to try to make her jealous); there is a sense of something unyielding and basic that cannot appeal to his sexual imagination, something far different from the girls who have been attracted by his tattoos. Above all, her eyes are "grey and sharp like the points of two ice-picks," an image that not only recalls his own gray microcosmic eyes but also the tattoo needle, which causes just enough pain to make the tattooing seem worthwhile. She complements his obsession with tattoos; whereas they suggest an egoistic but spiritual potency, she reveals his need for something firm outside himself, even something to which he may sacrifice himself in opposition to his common sense.

In trying to resolve both unsettling preoccupations, he decides to have a religious picture put on his back, the only spot remaining and, significantly, a spot where only she could see it, for it is really an offering to please his judge. The decision, almost the command, to have God's image placed there comes to him in an accident, when he runs a tractor into a tree, which bursts into flames like a fiery cross and burns up his shoes. His experience is described as a "leap forward into a worse unknown," a term made famous by Kierkegaard's description of the knight of faith in contrast to the esthetic or ethical man, but Parker continues to deny his motives and weakly to repudiate religion. The Byzantine Christ he chooses for his back has "all-demanding eyes" that make Sarah Ruth's seem soft and dilatory by comparison, since even her austerity is a comforting substitute for the absoluteness Parker desires and fears. When he returns home and reluctantly identifies himself through the barricaded door as "Obadiah," admitting to his given biblical name, he feels the light of the dawn "pouring through him, turning his spider web soul into a perfect arabesque of colors, a garden of trees and birds and beasts" (p. 243). His wife, however, repudiates the tattoo as idolatry and, having beaten the face of Christ, she drives Parker from the house to weep.

The ending of the story is complex in its possible implications. Sarah Ruth seems wrong in her rejection of incarnated God. Throughout, her disgust toward the body is as wrong as Parker's exaltation of it into an object of worship. Furthermore, Parker's religious experiences are intense, and they lead to that spiritual illumination in which his soul achieves the colorful harmony that his body had never achieved. There is still, however, some justice to Sarah Ruth's charge; it not only emphasizes the idolatrous nature of Parker's feelings about his images all along, but it also emphasizes that even when he is drawn close to God he still tries to evade the terrifying encounter by interposing his images, his pride, and his rationalizations. Even when he confronts the all-demanding eyes of Christ, he tries to hide behind his old idolatry and his wife, pretending that he is having this tattoo entirely to please her. Consequently, although his obsessions with tattoos and with his demanding wife both indicate capacity for faith and salvation, they also become convenient obstacles to faith when the part is mistaken for the whole, the symbols for the ultimate reality which they suggest.

In the main, however, Parker has begun to accept grace, which both elevates and humbles him. And in Miss O'Connor's fiction only grace can finally still the anxiety and longing that torment man. According to this Christian belief, only when man renounces his boast that he can save himself (a favorite boast of her characters), when he posits a power infinitely greater than, but not alien to, himself, when he can believe that he is accepted and can say with W. H. Auden's first man, "I am loved, therefore I am," only then can he achieve peace. Miss O'Connor's stories usually reach their climaxes and end with the violent beginnings of this new birth, or at least with the traumatic shock to the "old man" that makes the birth of the "new man" possible. Yet although she does not extend her stories much beyond the epiphanies toward which they have relentlessly moved, she does use minor characters throughout to suggest the harmony and peacefulness that her protagonists lack. As one would expect from an author who persistently criticized sentimentality, these characters are not entirely idealized; her sense of man's humanness and her sense of humor prevent even these foils from being flattened into easy perfection. Nevertheless, these redeemed characters do suggest the main qualities of a state of grace.

Amid all of the anxiety, avarice, and hatred in "The Displaced Person," Father Flynn, the eighty-year-old priest, floats with a gentle and often comic detachment. The down-to-earth women of the farm consider him to be in his second childhood because of his concern for the peacocks, which they consider a profitless nuisance: he gathers bouquets of feathers, feeds crumbs to the peacocks, stands in slack-jawed wonder before a bird with its feathers spread, and even likens it to the transfigured Christ. Although Father Flynn has arranged to have the displaced Poles come to work on Mrs. McIntyre's farm, he is most unworldly and has no conception of the practical and narrowly moralistic problems that bother Mrs. McIntyre about her immigrant workers. When she says that the Guizacs might leave her for more money, his answer is simple, but it shows him to be completely obtuse about the tight-fisted woman he is dealing with: " 'Arrrr, give them some morrre then,' he said indifferently. 'They have to get along' " (*Good Man*, p. 220). Later, when she has discovered Mr. Guizac's plan to marry his cousin to a Negro, Mrs. McIntyre complains violently to the priest that the Pole does not fit in, but Father Flynn merely reassures her that the Pole will learn to fit in, and he turns his attention to the peacocks. In part, the Jesuit often changes the subject because he is hurt and embarrassed by the woman's selfishness and practicality. He feels much more at ease speaking about the Redemption than about running a farm, and he is puzzled that other people are not humane. Mrs. McIntyre and Father Flynn are a comic pair; they misunderstand each other repeatedly; they talk at cross-purposes; they compete to push the conversation to either religious instruction or business complaints. In the end Father Flynn prevails, but not without a touch of lightly humorous irony. After Mrs. McIntyre has had a nervous breakdown and is bedridden, the priest visits her weekly to feed the peacocks and to explain the doctrines of the church to the captive and conquered woman.

Father Flynn's comic weaknesses are merely the practical deficiencies of his spiritual wisdom, as is true of the nuns in "A Temple of the Holy Ghost," for the wisdom of God is often the foolishness of man. Like the peacocks, the old priest seems useless, because he is not concerned with utility. He does not try frantically to build defenses against nothing or to stuff himself with symbols of plenitude. Since he knows that Christ came to redeem us, he is essentially, if absent-mindedly, at peace.

Father Flynn is a stock character, a lovable, childlike man with a deeper wisdom than sensibleness allows. This, together with his being a priest, makes it easy to see that his faults are venial. The problem is much more difficult, however, with the mother in "The Comforts of Home," for she is a character of unforced natural goodness with all the charity, confusion, and spiritual limitations of the symbolic child of nature. The plot is very simple in this story, which is one of Miss O'Connor's least ambitious. The mother takes care of a psychopathic delinquent girl; the "intellectual" son, Thomas, detests the girl and tries to keep his mother from making a fool of herself. He plots to have the girl arrested for stealing his pistol, but he accidentally kills his mother, who interposes herself in a scuffle between the two. The mother quite definitely lacks sound judgment and a realistic understanding of evil. Also, she is not very bright and can express herself only through habitual platitudes that irritate her educated son. Above all, her charity is rather "hazy," as her son claims; it is sentimental and confused, since it comes from vague feelings that lack a religious center. In this regard she differs radically from Father Flynn, whom she resembles emotionally and morally. Unlike the priest, she is outside the body of the church, and her charity does not proceed, as does his, from faith in God's love and in the Redemption. Her good intentions are clumsy and ineffective, for Miss O'Connor is pointedly didactic on the limits of natural virtue. In her *Memoir of Mary Ann* she wrote that, "In the absence of this faith now, we govern by tenderness. It is a tenderness which, long since cut off from the person of Christ, is wrapped in theory. When tenderness is detached from the source of tenderness, its logical outcome is terror" (*Mystery and Manners*, p. 227). Although the mother's tenderness is not wrapped in theory, not so much a matter of sociology and politics, it is clearly detached from any source beyond itself, and it ends in a mixture of terror and slapstick.

Given these qualities, one could easily find a place for her among Miss O'Connor's strongly satirical characters: with the self-deluding social workers who are good but not right, or with Mrs. Turpin, who never spares herself to do good deeds for others, or with many of the cheery and platitudinous farm women who drive their intellectual children nearly crazy. One commentator, in fact, has claimed that she has a "tragically shallow nature" because her good will, although genuine, is ill-conceived and because she does not understand that the delinquent young woman is a thoroughly depraved person.[3]

But to stop with these characteristics and consider the woman a well-meaning, shallow fool who thinks that evil comes from one's lack of a good home is to miss too much of the character; *mutatis mutandis,* she has the natural virtues of Father Flynn, who also was naive about evil and most unpractical in his humanity (he too, as a matter of fact, helped to bring about a pathetic death because he was not worldly enough in his knowledge of people). First, Miss O'Connor's descriptions indicate that the woman is something more than a misguided fool. When the son says to her in exasperation, "Can't I make you see . . . that if she can't help herself you can't help her," the narrator comments, "His mother's eyes, intimate but untouchable, were the blue of great distances after sunset" (*Everything*, p. 117). To some extent this far-sightedness is an ironic sign of the woman's inability to see things that are nearby and obvious, but the image is commonly used in Miss O'Connor's stories to signify spiritual vision, the ability to see things with their added dimension. Later, when she is quite worried about the girl, the mother comes to breakfast in a bathrobe and gray turban, "which gave her face a disconcerting omniscient look. He might have been breakfasting with a sibyl" (p. 127). Of course, this sibyl is concerned with coffee cream and she is hardly omniscient, but again the irony is less important than the suggestion of her vague special insight.

The more specific comments about her feelings and actions justify these images. She speaks in clichés, but we are told that "there were real experiences behind them," a fact which differentiates her from the trite, satirical characters who use clichés to avoid experiences. Above all, she gives her love and compassion freely, completely, and unselfishly. Unlike the demonic altruists of other stories, she is not self-righteous; she is not a miser of good works; and she does not show the underlying anxiety or the mechanical gestures of the demonic. Her love for her son at times becomes "pure idiot mystery and he sensed about him forces, invisible currents entirely out of his control" (which recalls Rayber's uncontrollable love for his son in *The Violent Bear It Away*), and she extends her symbolic motherhood to include the girl, even though her feeling is expressed in the cliché that her son might have been born like that female psychopath. The old lady's compassion (her "suffering with") even becomes universal in scope. After the girl, Sarah Ham, has feigned a suicide attempt, the narrator comments about the mother:

> Some new weight of sorrow seemed to have been thrown across her shoulders, and not only Thomas, but Sarah Ham was infuriated by this, for it appeared to be a general sorrow that would have found another object no matter what good fortune came to either of them. The experience of Sarah Ham had plunged the old lady into mourning for the world. (p. 133)

Again, there is a play of humor in the comment, but the character is not to be seen as a self-indulgent melancholic, seeking objects of pity. Through the despair of the girl and her son, she comes to suffer for the despair of mankind, although she cannot interpret her feeling or define its ultimate context.

It is appropriate to the essence of the character and her symbolic meaning that her sorrow becomes general in import and yet remains personal and attached to specific suffering. She does not care for mankind in the abstract; she does not delude herself, as do Miss O'Connor's social workers, by trying to love faceless statistics. Her feelings are intense and personal, therefore, specific. But, ironically, they are also indiscriminate and almost disinterested. She loves because Sarah Ham *is* and needs love, not because the girl is worthy of being loved or because the old lady will benefit from loving her. In a sentence quoted earlier, the mother's eyes are described as "intimate but untouchable," a phrase which points to this strange combination of attitudes. It also describes the paradoxical nature of the Christian God, whose morality she embodies. One could further extend the allegorical implications of this woman, who literally sacrifices her life to save the depraved girl, but the story deals in suggestions, not coherent allegories. Instead, I believe that while the character is in many trying ways an irritating mother and a naive, confused sentimentalist, she is also a woman of the highest natural virtue, one who can accept others because she has accepted herself. Thus, like Father Flynn, she is somewhat remote and peaceful in herself, yet by no means dispassionate toward others.

Appropriately, both Sarah Ham and Thomas are angered that the mother offers love so freely and abundantly, and they feel insulted and threatened because their precarious independence is challenged. But they are flat characters (as in a different way are Father Flynn and the mother), which is not to say that they are entirely simple but that they do not develop, they do not surprise. The main characters of most of the stories, however, do progress to an awareness of their need for mercy, and these progressions constitute the action of the stories. I do not mean only that Miss O'Connor's characters begin at one spiritual and psychological point and end up at another. I mean that the characters *move* between those points—they are not merely picked up and transported by an authorial angel—and the main preoccupation is with that movement, not with the theological, psychological, and social insights that help to form it. The epiphanies in "Revelation" and "The Enduring Chill" are well grounded in the psychology of the characters but not determined by it. There is a qualitative leap but also a culmination, a gesture, that is free but appropriate, and the sense that grace is given but also accepted. I also contend that this movement is grounded in the structure as well as the psychology of the stories, because Miss O'Connor's religious beliefs reinforce, rather than conflict with, her craftsmanship. In praising her representation of natural and supernatural grace, Caroline Gordon writes, ". . . she has a firmer grasp of the architectonics of fiction than any of her contemporaries." [4]

"The Artificial Nigger," which, like "Revelation" and "The Enduring Chill," has been criticized for ending with an unjustified religious insight, is so carefully structured that it is nearly an archetypal comedy. The basic comic form, according to critics of literature as myth and ritual, is a pattern of symbolic death and rebirth, a completed redemptive action.[5] Comedy begins with hypocrisy, illusion, and compulsiveness; it moves through a process of unmasking, often with a release of repressed Dionysian or even demonic forces; and it concludes by establishing a new order that is saner and more harmonious than the original one. The central *agon*, which often occupies most of the comedy, frequently involves a descent into a demonic realm of darkness and labyrinths, the expulsion of a boasting pretender (the *alazon*), and a ritualistic death or at least an approach to it. The general pattern, then, is ostensibly a circle, since there is frequently a return to the initial setting and social order, but it is actually more of a spiral, since the initial order has become revitalized and more flexible.

"The Artificial Nigger" fits this pattern and has many of the specific actions, symbols, and themes of the mythic comic genre. The story begins, as it will end, in the transforming light of the moon:

> After a second, he saw half of the moon five feet away in his shaving mirror, paused as if it were waiting for his permission to enter. It rolled forward and cast a dignifying look on everything. The straight chair against the wall looked stiff and attentive as if it were awaiting an order and Mr. Head's trousers, hanging to the back of it, had an almost noble air, like the garment some great man had just flung to his servant, but the face on the moon was a grave one. (*Good Man*, p. 102)

The significance of the light is twofold, and it is also ironic. It faintly suggests a true illumination whereby the ordinary surfaces of the world are transformed by mystery, but this meaning is latent only and will not fully emerge until the conclusion of the story when the characters have been prepared to receive such revelation. In the beginning they are far too egoistic to recognize this mystery, and so the moonlight becomes an instrument in their own self-deception. For Mr. Head the moonlit scene is but another tribute to his own grandeur. The center of his pride is his belief that with age he has achieved "that calm understanding of life that makes him a suitable guide for the young," specifically for his grandson, Nelson, with whom he has continual petty contests to show that his wisdom and experience are superior to the cantankerous child's. The boy feels that he has the irrevocable advantage of having been born in the city, so the old man has arranged a trip there to humble his grandson once and for all. He will show him that there is no cause to be proud of being born in such a place; he will make him content to spend the rest of his days in the country; and he will demonstrate his own indispensability as a guide to the ignorant boy, who has never been on a railroad or seen a Negro.

The journey turns out to be a symbolic descent into hell for the boy and his inadequate Virgil. The demonic nature of the city is implied most clearly by the sewer system, which the old man explains to frighten the boy. Nelson connects the sewers with the entrances to hell and understands "for the first time how the world was put together in its lower parts" (pp. 115–16). The darkness, the labyrinthine tunnels, the frightening unknown, even the slight hint of sexuality implied by "lower parts" will all become characteristics of the city itself, as they are characteristics of the mythic wasteland or nightmare world through which the comic heroes travel toward rebirth. It is not long before Mr. Head, trying to show that he knows his way around, gets them both lost and strays into a Negro neighborhood. They grow increasingly nervous as they wander, watched from all sides by black eyes in black faces, until finally Nelson gets up the courage to ask directions from a large black woman, despite the warning to beware of dark women which he has received from a comically sibylline weighing machine. His experience is overwhelming, showing in its violent release of unknown passions that the demonic world into which they have journeyed partly represents their own demonic natures which suddenly erupt to break their feelings of self-control:

> His eyes traveled up from her great knees to her forehead and then made a triangular path from the glistening sweat on her neck down and across her tremendous bosom and over her bare arm to where her fingers lay hidden in her hair. He suddenly wanted her to reach down and pick him up and draw him against her and then he wanted to feel her breath on his face. He wanted to look down and down into her eyes while she held him tighter and tighter. He had never had such a feeling before. He felt as if he were reeling down through a pitchblack tunnel. (p. 119)

Whereas before he had recoiled in fascinated terror from the dark, gurgling sewers, he now correspondingly longs to be pulled into a parallel darkness, to lose himself in a pitchblack tunnel. The explicit sexuality, with its suggestions of the dark mother enfolding her child, seems at first a strange intrusion into a story in which there is little preparation for, or subsequent development of, a sexual theme. But the experience is nevertheless valid in the mythic pattern; when the lord of misrule breaks the social or psychological order, bringing about either a festive or destructive comic release, there is usually an eruption of repressed erotic forces such as this boy's unsuspected desires. Miss O'Connor later dealt more extensively with the theme in "Greenleaf," where she developed the connections among sexuality, the desire to destroy the repressive self, and a sublimated longing for the infinite. Here, she briefly touches upon the subject, but implies its meanings through the symbolic connections of this scene and other incidents in this demonic journey.

When they begin to follow streetcar tracks back toward the railroad station, they seem about to escape from their dark imprisonment. However, when Nelson falls asleep during a rest stop on this walk, the insecure Mr. Head, whose authority has been damaged by the trip, decides to teach Nelson another lesson by hiding from him. The boy awakens alone, runs down the street in panic, and collides with an old woman who claims to have suffered a broken ankle and calls for the police. Surrounded by a crowd of strange women and terrified at the thought of the police, Mr. Head denies his own image and likeness and claims he has never seen the boy before. The shocked women allow the man and the boy to leave, but the treachery has broken the relationship between them, leaving the old man in disgrace and loneliness, cut off from the only thing outside of himself that he cares for. For the lost and lonely old man the scene becomes entirely a wasteland: the street seems a "hollow tunnel," the houses are "partially submerged icebergs," the drives wind around like "endless ridiculous circles," and as the sun sets there is no one else in sight in the elegant suburb they have entered. Finally, the grandfather sees a passerby, and he shouts out his literal and metaphorical confession: "Oh Gawd

I'm lost! Oh hep me Gawd I'm lost!" (p. 126). Given directions, they proceed toward a train station, but Nelson no longer cares about home, and Mr. Head knows now "what time would be like without seasons and heat would be like without light and what man would be like without salvation" (p. 127). This state is a symbolic hell, a feeling of complete estrangement from God, which is also an estrangement from others and oneself. The *alazon* of this story, the boasting pretender in Mr. Head (and to some extent in Nelson) has been defeated and cast out, leaving for the moment the despair of recognized emptiness. Miss O'Connor frequently ends her stories at this point, when the "old man" has been destroyed and the advent of the "new man" made more probable. In this story she completes the comic pattern and, with a second climax, brings about the rebirth.

No other incident in Miss O'Connor's work is so complex and ironic in its implications, so resistant to a simple allegorical reading, and yet so symbolically precise as this second reversal. The two characters come upon a plaster lawn statue of a Negro, who looks too miserable to be young or old: "He was meant to look happy because his mouth was stretched up at the corners but the chipped eye and the angle he was cocked at gave him a wild look of misery instead" (p. 127). Confronted by what seems to them "some great mystery, some monument to another's victory that brought them together in their common defeat," they are reconciled, and Mr. Head feels what mercy is. Probably the most common interpretation of this scene is that the statue is a sign which shows the characters that all men are incomplete and suffering. The point seems valid, since Nelson is thereby relieved of his self-righteous resentment and Mr. Head's preoccupation with his suffering is relaxed. Yet this reading does not exhaust the suggestiveness of the scene. Mercy involves compassion and forgiveness, which in Christianity are centered in the Crucifixion and Redemption, and this symbolic agent of mercy suggests Christ, who took upon himself man's sin and pain. Thus, Mr. Head and Nelson would sense not only that all men are as the figure but also that God, too, became that chipped and miserable creature, man. The characters' recognition of their own inadequacies is only part of the process toward the final religious insights; they must also be able to believe that they are accepted, although unworthy. Mr. Head has already undergone a sacrifice of his proud self in this comic pattern of death and rebirth. Now he must also sense the sacrifice made for him by God, who became a scapegoat to enable man's rebirth. The characters cannot fully analyze what they sense in the experience, and their explanations are oblique, while revealing. When Nelson seems to implore his grandfather to explain once and for all the mystery of existence, the old man tries to seem wise and hears himself say, " 'They ain't got enough real ones here. They got to have an artificial one' " (p. 128). Suiting Mr. Head's character, the explanation is given in terms of his fear and scorn of Negroes and of city people who live with them. But at a deeper level, of which he is certainly not conscious, it also scorns those who make idols of man's own broken nature, and increase man's suffering. Thus, the statue has many conflicting meanings for them, for they have many conflicting attitudes, including religious insights and demonic fears. The statue is for them a symbol of incomplete man and of redeeming God; it is the mystery in existence which they have tried to deny in their arrogance but which has defeated them through the city, the dark woman, and their own submerged impulses; it is the epitome of the city itself with its idolatry, loneliness, and misery; and it is the object of Mr. Head's superstitious, fearful bigotry, which comes from his insecurity and pride.

When the old man and the boy return home, the moon again has been "restored to its full splendor," and Mr. Head no longer fancies it to be heightening his grandeur. Instead, as he is again touched by mercy, he understands that "no sin was too monstrous for him to claim as his own," that God's mercy grows out of agony, and that he is "forgiven for sins from the beginning of time" (p. 129). Experiencing the greatness of God's love and forgiveness, he feels ready to enter paradise. Miss O'Connor's religious exposition is, in itself, very well done, but it does seem too articulate and too theologically precise for Mr. Head. This is not to say that his central insights into his own sinfulness, God's mercy, and his sudden elation are unjustified by the rest of the story. Miss O'Connor is not arbitrarily manipulating her character and plot to suit her belief in grace. The fault is much less important; she is merely formulating those insights better than Mr. Head could do and in contexts of which he has not shown any awareness before; she is yielding to the temptation to address the reader through her characters and to explain what he senses but could not so thoroughly explain. The fault is a slight matter of point of view, for as Gordon has written, "When Miss O'Connor falls short of her best work, the flaw is always in the execution of the story, not in its structure." [6]

In fact, the final insights are not only justified by the whole story, they are demanded by it. Psychologically, Mr. Head and Nelson, despite their bravado, are desperately insecure throughout. Despite their claims to be in control, they have persistent feelings of awe, fear, and wonder; despite their feigned independence, they are very dependent on each other. After his pride has been destroyed, Mr. Head becomes aware of these feelings and his sinful denial of them, and he sees them in religious terms, which are in effect the ultimate terms in which these psychological and moral questions can be formulated. Structurally, the conclusion fulfills the basic comic pattern. After an *agon* of confusion, passion, unmasking, and despair, Mr. Head returns home with greater humanity and awareness. He is no longer as comically compulsive or as demonically bound, since the chaotic release has brought about a higher order. He is no longer so estranged from himself, so distorted by imbalanced and unrecognized impulses; nor is he as estranged from Nelson, whom he had loved but whom he also had used as an object for his own pride; nor is he as estranged from God, for whom he had not felt a need. The conclusion of mythic comedy and the working of grace both bring not only greater joy, but also an expanded sense of reality, greater harmony, and a freer, more complete humanity.

Critics who have objected to Miss O'Connor's handling of divine grace, however, have not all thought that the stories lacked adequate preparation for it. More often they have found her conclusions too determined and have claimed that the characters do not turn to God through their free will. Related to this objection is the claim that, when the characters do accept God, they further sacrifice their freedom and their individual identities. Although these problems are most often raised in connection with the novels, they are intrinsic to the present subject of grace and its action and effects in the stories.

I have insisted that the main acts of accepting grace are both surprising leaps in perception and gestures appropriate to the characters. To take one more instance, I will consider a climactic gesture mentioned earlier, the grandmother's acceptance of The Misfit in "A Good Man Is Hard to Find." As The Misfit orders his men to kill her family, the old lady becomes terrified and nearly hysterical, but The Misfit also becomes more upset as he talks about Jesus and his own distorted nature. Suddenly, the revelation occurs,

> His voice seemed about to crack and the grandmother's head cleared for an instant. She saw the man's face twisted close to her own as if he were going to cry and she murmured, "Why you're one of my babies. You're one of my own children!" She reached out and touched him on the shoulder. The Misfit sprang back as if a snake had bitten him and shot her three times through the chest. (*Good Man*, p. 29)

Her recognition suits her persistent and often irritating grandmotherliness. Throughout the family's trip she has tried to entertain, educate, and manage her ornery grandchildren, even though they have scorned her trite but affectionate attempts. She has a doting fondness for her cat, which she smuggles into the car for fear that it would miss her and perhaps asphyxiate itself by accidentally brushing a gas burner. And, as they pass a Negro's shack, she gushes sentimentally about a "cute little pickaninny," whose picture she would paint if she knew how. She is thus established early in the story as a doting mother to children, cats, and pickaninnies. These attitudes are shown mainly to be ridiculous in their sentimentality and condescension, but they do come from a real, if distorted, capacity for affection. Her recognition of The Misfit as one of her babies is partly an extension of this capacity. It is, however, more than a quantitative extension; it is a leap of perception. She does not accept him because he is part of her literal family, or cute like a pickaninny, or because he is a "good man," or "comes from nice people," or is "nice" like people used to be, which up to that moment had been her main standards; she accepts him because he is suffering and, although he will not admit it, needs that acceptance. As the motives for, and objects of, her love change, so does the quality of that love. It becomes agape, and, as with the mother of "The Comforts of Home," there are faint suggestions of the Crucifixion as the grandmother lies "in a puddle of blood with her legs crossed under her like a child's and her face smiling up at the cloudless sky" (p. 29). From The Misfit's point of view, the association between the old lady and Christ is emphatic: He recoils from her touch and forgiveness because it challenges the obsessive defiance of God he strains to preserve; he kills her as another rejection of Jesus. From an objective point of view, her illumination is a natural sign of grace; such love, like faith and hope, are possible only through God's mercy.

The problem of the free but appropriate act, which is exemplified by the grandmother's insight, is partly a question of how grace works through nature without destroying it, and Miss O'Connor's beliefs as a Christian humanist on this matter help to shape her handling of the climax, even though the theme of grace is not explicit in this story. But the problem also involves the nature of man's self, a subject that is more obviously relevant even to those works in which the characters' relations to God are not made explicit. Kierkegaard is again helpful on such a problem of religious psychology. He claims that within man's dialectical self, just as infinitude is limited by finitude, so possibility is limited by necessity: "Inasmuch as [the self] is itself, it is the necessary, and inasmuch as it has to become itself, it is a possibility." [7] This dialectical nature has been denied by many existential atheists, who claim that man has no essence, no necessity, that he is entirely free to make himself, that he is, in effect, a process of continuous becoming. For Kierkegaard this is the despair of possibility, in which "more and more things become possible, because nothing becomes actual," in which "the self runs away from itself" and "what is really lacking is the power to obey, to submit to the necessary in oneself, to what may be called one's limit." This analysis is useful, for it provides a new approach to the traditional Christian doctrine that man's true freedom is in his acceptance of God and of his own essence. If man has an essential self, he cannot live freely in opposition to it; if he could, "freedom" would mean only freedom of choice, unlimited possibility. And such a state would be a nightmare of illusions in which nothing was real or definite, in which reality was merely a momentary choice, subject to continual reversal. It would be the despair of The Misfit, and Miss O'Connor knew how illusory is such freedom in which "nothing becomes actual." (In this regard, consider how inactive and ineffectual are her characters who think that they are free intellectual skeptics.) She forms her characters convincingly out of an awareness of man's dialectical nature and out of the belief that the truly free act does not violate man's essential self nor is it irrelevant to the existential self of the person.

The dialectical nature of man is also relevant to the problem of man's individual identity. Several theologians and psychologists have distinguished between individuality and personality, claiming that the former term overly stresses uniqueness, difference, and separateness, whereas the latter also considers commonality and relationship. It is hardly surprising that, in reaction to mass society and its superficial standardizing, many people have come to consider individuality as an end in itself, but it is no more valuable in itself than is its opposite, and pursuing it excessively is as destructive as prohibiting it. Thus, it is also not surprising that the problems of reconciling individuality and commonality, egoism and self-sacrifice, *animus* and *anima*, have been central in modern intellectual history. Consider, for example, how many poets and novelists of the past century and a half have been preoccupied with these reconciliations. Miss O'Connor, too, is preoccupied with them, from a Christian point of view. It would be wrong to assume that she does not value individuality because she does not confuse it with the whole person, because she recognizes that complete individuality, if it were possible, would be complete estrangement, or damnation. The whole person, who is also the free person, can exist only within the limits of the necessary in himself and in the rest of existence. The state of grace is an ideal of reconciled and harmonious impulses, and the acceptance of grace is a centered act of the personality in which possibility and necessity, independence and dependence, are brought into balance.

Miss O'Connor, however, recognized two important dangers in religious awakenings, and if one does not see that she was quite aware of those dangers, one can easily distort her conceptions of faith and grace, as critics have done most often with *The Violent Bear It Away*. She knew that despair could lead to a demonic rather than a divine revelation and that the supposed "new man" could be actually a false prophet, either bringing a demonic message or, more subtly, using divine

truths for demonic purposes. The false believer has not overcome despair; he has come near to insight but has found a
way to avoid faith without realizing it. He has not been
willing to take the final steps of sacrificing his pride and his
coveted independence and so has managed to continue self-
worship while appearing to have been enlightened.

The most clearly developed case of demonic revelation
is that of Mrs. Shortley in "The Displaced Person." In the
opening of the story this wife of the hired dairyman seems to
be a fully stable philistine who stands "on two tremendous
legs, with the grand self-confidence of a mountain" and who
has no interest in such unpractical things as a peacock's tail
that looks like a map of the universe. She considers religion
to be, at best, "a social occasion providing the opportunity
to sing," and she is scornful of Father Flynn and his unre-
formed church. But the coming of the displaced Poles begins
to unsettle Mrs. Shortley. Practically, she is afraid that the
Guizacs have come over to replace good, nearly honest American workers. She talks of the replacement of the Negroes, but
as she finds out how valuable a worker Mr. Guizac is, she
begins unconsciously to worry about her own place. Less ra-
tionally, she also feels threatened by their foreign speech,
manners, and religion. Recalling a newsreel showing a heap
of dead bodies in a concentration camp, she begins to associate the Guizacs with the murderous ways of Europe, where
people are "not as advanced as we are." In one of Miss
O'Connor's excellent brief insights, Mrs. Shortley confounds
the victims of an appalling evil with the evil itself, a common confusion in which the victims begin to seem guilty because they have suffered so much and because they have been
vaguely involved with a persecution too overwhelming for
analysis.

As her anxiety grows, Mrs. Shortley becomes aware for
the first time that there are more things on heaven and earth
than she has dreamt of. She becomes aware of the devil, but
she mistakenly thinks that Mr. Guizac is his representative.

Out of fear and hatred of the displaced person, she begins reading her Bible, particularly the Apocalypse and the Prophets, and she comes to feel that she has reached "a deeper understanding of her existence." She sees that the meaning of the world is a mystery and that she is one of the strong ones chosen to play a special part in the divine plan. Then one Sunday afternoon she has a vision:

> Suddenly while she watched, the sky folded back in two pieces like the curtain to a stage and a gigantic figure stood facing her. It was the color of the sun in the early afternoon, white-gold. It was of no definite shape but there were fiery wheels with fierce dark eyes in them, spinning rapidly all around it. She was not able to tell if the figure was going forward or backward because its magnificence was so great. She shut her eyes in order to look at it and it turned blood-red and the wheels turned white. A voice, very resonant, said the one word, "Prophesy!"
>
> She stood there, tottering slightly but still upright, her eyes shut tight and her fists clenched and her straw sun hat low on her forehead. "The children of wicked nations will be butchered," she said in a loud voice. "Legs where arms should be, foot to face, ear in the palm of hand. Who will remain whole? Who?" (*Good Man*, pp. 218–19)

With imagistic help from Ezekiel and the newsreel, Mrs. Shortley has called herself to prophesy. She has summoned up a vision to justify her hatred, to flatter her pride, and to subdue her impotent fears. She has assumed righteousness and distinguished herself from the wicked whom she condemns, thus violating what Tillich has described as the role of the true prophet: "Isaiah exhibits profound insight, when he identifies himself with his unclean people in the very moment that he is made worthy of his exceptional vision. . . . For even in the greatest ecstasy, a prophet does not forget the social group to which he belongs, and its unclean character which he cannot lose." [8] But in her self-imputed righteousness Mrs. Shortley cannot admit her share of guilt in the persecution that she is helping to continue; in fact, in referring to "the children of wicked nations," she even gives her prophecy the arrogantly nationalistic sense which many Christian theologians criticize as demonic literalism in Old Testament prophecy. And most obviously, she dwells upon vengeance and destruction, ironically ignoring the clouds that look "like rows and rows of white fish," suggesting Christ's mercy and the Redemption.

Mrs. Shortley does not have her vengeance, because her practical fears come true and her family is ousted by the smarter, more energetic Guizacs. But as the defeated woman, who has become a displaced person herself, drives off with her possessions, she has another revelation, but this one destroys her pride and shows her "for the first time the tremendous frontier of her true country" (p. 223). She struggles to resist the vision of her emptiness: she clutches to herself everything she can reach—her husband's head, her daughter's leg, the cat, bedding, her own knee—as if to prevent what is hers from slipping away and to fill her emptiness by ingesting the whole world. This climactic experience, which ends in a stroke and her death, recalls her prophecy of mangled bodies and ironically helps to answer her prophetic question, "Who will remain whole? Who?"

Miss O'Connor did not again create such a clear pattern of false revelation, clarified and corrected by true revelation, but she did create many characters who have elements of the false prophet. The Misfit is intensely aware of spiritual problems, but he has chosen to worship himself rather than accept Christ. Rufus Johnson, the juvenile delinquent in "The Lame Shall Enter First," knows the reality of Satan and Jesus, and he knows that a person must testify to one or the other, but with the pride of the nonelect he claims that he is "in Satan's power." So, his scornful statement, "when I get ready to be saved, Jesus'll save me," is an egoistic parody of spiritual freedom, as his grotesque claim to salvation demonstrates: "The lame'll carry off the prey!" Even characters who are devout worshipers of Christ may confound their faith with superstition, self-righteousness, and hatred. The experiences of dread, spiritual awareness, and even religious intensity are not adequate signs that man is free of the demonic. Despite the apparent simplicity of conversion suggested by some of her violent climaxes, Miss O'Connor realized that faith is as complex a problem as man's nature.

The second danger of religious awakening is the assumption that a true revelatory experience is complete. This implication, too, comes largely from the violent conclusions of Miss O'Connor's stories, which seem to suggest that her characters' epiphanies transform them entirely. But this belief would conflict with her general view of man's imperfection and with the Catholic doctrine derived from Paul that the "old man" must be continuously put off through a continuous renewal, that the new freedom received from the Spirit is repeatedly limited by sin. We are told that Asbury of "The Enduring Chill" will live "for the rest of his days . . . in the face of a purifying terror." And when the child in a "A Temple of the Holy Ghost" realizes that all men are temples, she is not thereby transformed into a saint; she still has ugly thoughts about the nun she meets, and she notices that the fat cab driver has pointed ears like a pig. Also, considered in these terms, The Misfit's final statement about the grandmother takes on particular significance; after she has made her Christ-like offering and been killed, he says, "She would have been a good woman, if it had been somebody there to shoot her every minute of her life." As Miss O'Connor said, "in us the good is something under construction" (*Mystery and Manners*, p. 226); so, not even the acceptance of grace completes man's nature for the rest of his life. He still remains free, and by faith, hope, love, and the gift of grace he must continuously overcome despair.

Finally, although it is seldom an explicit theme in the stories, one might suggest that for Miss O'Connor these awakenings can only be fully realized within the body of the church and through the sacraments. From her specifically Catholic point of view, which is stated throughout her letters and lectures and implied in several of her stories, the subjective stirrings of self-awareness and Christian faith are completed only by membership in the visible church. Therefore, the sacramental symbols that pervade her work not only suggest personal spiritual relations, but they also point toward the literal vehicles of grace by which the subjective states are fulfilled. Usually, however, this position is only slightly apparent in the backgrounds of her stories. As an author, she is concerned far more with the drama of the religious individual than with the Christian body.

4. The Arc and the Circle:
Wise Blood and
The Violent Bear It Away

*I*n her two novels, *Wise Blood* and *The Violent Bear It Away*, Flannery O'Connor deals with all of the problems I have discussed in relation to her stories, and she makes her religious preoccupations still more explicit, although sometimes more complex. *Wise Blood*, however, has often been criticized for being an exotic book. Even some of its readers who recognize allegorical outlines have objected that it is the story of an unrepresentative Everyman on a special, not universal, quest. I think that the main problems of the novel are quite the opposite. Despite the heavily exotic and grotesque incidents, descriptions, and minor characters, Miss O'Connor has been too ambitious in her themes and has tried to write almost a survey of major spiritual, psychological, and social problems. Consequently, her novel is too diffuse; it sometimes is too ambiguous as it tries to make situations serve conflicting purposes; and it is several times too pat in its use of social and religious platitudes. Nevertheless, these weaknesses, which are common to first novels, come not from regional or religious parochialism, but from a broad and complex interest in mankind.

Wise Blood is the story of Hazel Motes, who tries violently to repudiate his fundamentalist background but who finally accepts his guilt and redemption. Although in her preface to the second edition Miss O'Connor corrected some early misunderstanding by announcing that Haze's integrity lay in his not being able to get rid of Christ, her presentation of his religious impulses is still ambiguous. The problem centers on Haze's attitudes toward salvation when he was a child, and it derives primarily from Miss O'Connor's attempt to use those attitudes for opposing ends. Haze's mother was a stern, black-robed woman who impressed upon him a sense of his guiltiness, and his grandfather was a circuit preacher who shouted to his listeners about the soul-hungry Jesus who pursued sinners, particularly "that mean sinful unthinking boy standing there." In part, the child's resulting mixture of fear, awe, and longing is a desirable contrast to the spiritual indifference and complacency found in almost every other character in the book. It does not smooth down religious experience into a sweet, sentimental evasion of God, as does the bogus religion of Onnie Jay Holy, the street preacher and con man who reassures people that they are basically "roses of sweetness," that they do not have to believe anything they do not understand, and that for one dollar they can join his church and overcome loneliness and despair. The Jesus about which young Haze is taught is a mystery; He demands that one must lose one's life in order to gain it; and He offers himself in a dreadful sacrifice for mankind, whom He claims as his own. Given the context of the secular society in which Haze will move, one can hardly doubt that Miss O'Connor is dramatizing some of the qualities that she believes are necessary for a true encounter with God. Since she knows that her audience does not hold her beliefs, she must use shock ("to the hard of hearing you shout, and for the almost-blind you draw large and startling figures" [*Mystery and Manners*, p. 34]), but she is not just exaggerating religious feelings for a rhetorical effect or simply approving of Haze's Christianity while disapproving of his fanaticism.

She believes that to love God sincerely is sometimes to fear Him, to try to flee from Him, to feel guilt and dread. She presents Haze's awe and terror as a necessary part of Christianity when it has not been quieted into a comforting "souls-ease."

But Miss O'Connor is also criticizing Haze's attitudes, not because they are extreme or violent, but because they are morbid and Manichean, a contrast to the Christian-humanistic position that she assumes throughout her work. The boy does not basically fear guiltiness or damnation, nor does he fear a God of wrath and vengeance; he fears Jesus. ("There was already a deep black wordless conviction in him that the way to avoid Jesus was to avoid sin.") [1] And he fears Jesus not as the Judge who separaes the sheep from the goats, but as the Redeemer who, as the grandfather says, would chase the boy over the waters of sin to keep him from losing his soul. He sees Jesus as a devourer—"soul-hungry" in the grandfather's words—and salvation as destruction of himself, as being eaten, drowned, or drawn into the uncertain darkness. In a sense, even this conception of Jesus is partly valid. It indicates that He is the tiger as well as the lamb and that, as Miss O'Connor demonstrates repeatedly in her works, even God's mercy burns as it purifies and makes worthy. But Haze's conception goes further: it requires a complete scorn of the world and of the self, and it will tolerate no relation with God short of a mystical consummation. It is one aspect of what Miss O'Connor recognized as "the Manichean spirit of the times" (*Mystery and Manners*, p. 33), and it opposes her sacramental view of existence. In the short stories there are several echoes of such Manicheism, as in Sarah Ruth ("Parker's Back"), who rejects an incarnated God as idolatry, or Mrs. May ("Greenleaf"), whose initial self-control recoils into a symbolic self-destruction in union with the Bull-God.

It is true that the Christian is expected to sacrifice his independence and the proud self of the old Adam within him, but he does so to find his essential self, not to be destroyed and gathered into a mystical oneness. As D'Arcy explains as the central thesis of *The Mind and the Heart of Love*, the fullest love that the Christian feels for God has a balance of the "egocentric" and "ecstatic" forces which were imbalanced in the Fall. It is also true that the Christian is required to renounce the world, but he does so to have it given back transfigured, to find it the creation and vessel of God. Kierkegaard explains this best as the central paradox of the knight of faith who, in "infinite resignation" abandons all claim to the world, who hates his family and his own life (as commanded in Luke 14:26), and yet who believes by virtue of the impossible that all will be given to him. He is Abraham, who is about to kill Isaac but who still believes that Isaac will not be taken from him.[2] But the young Hazel Motes is no Abraham in his religion. For him, to accept redemption is to renounce the world without the final stage of faith that trusts God as did Abraham. Haze is torn by fear and longing. He is a "Jesus hog," as a false street preacher later calls him, but he is also afraid to abandon the familiar things around him to enter the darkness. He wants the redemption that he conceives as death, but he also fears it.

From the beginning of the novel, Haze is haunted by the idea of death. The first chapter describes his responses to the burials of four members of his family, and in each case he is terrified by the thought of being entombed. He keeps thinking that the dead people are going to outwit death and escape the dark coffins; as a child, he imagined that his grandfather would stick his elbow into the crack to keep the lid from closing tight, and long after his parents' deaths he dreams that his dead father had "humped over on his hands and knees in his coffin" to keep the lid open and that his mother had become a bat to fly out. But there is no outwitting the grave, and the coffin lids close down tight. Haze dreams of his father's and mother's burials while he is lying in a pullman berth, which in his half sleep he takes to be his own coffin and from which he tries desperately to escape.

Miss O'Connor does not schematize these attitudes toward death into an easy formula. In fact, the significances of Haze's feelings are as conflicting as the feelings themselves. Despite important psychological patterns, one must not forget that Haze's concern with death is in part a necessary religious preoccupation with last things, which most of the characters in the novel ignore as if their lives were unending. Miss O'Connor writes later that "the creative action of a Christian's life is to prepare his death in Christ" (*Mystery and Manners*, p. 223), and she says often that, as a Catholic, she naturally considers death an appropriate ending for her stories. It would be wrong, then, to think of Haze's concern only as morbidity or as an abnormal fear resulting from his childhood experiences with death and religion; to do so would be to accept the point of view of Miss O'Connor's grotesquely shallow rationalists. If one does admit the religious value of his preoccupation, one may also see his dreams as an unrecognized desire for redemption to overcome death, to escape from the coffin. This is indicated by the brief scene that ends chapter one, as Haze awakens, screaming and cursing, in his coffin-berth:

"I'm sick!" he called. "I can't be closed up in this thing. Get me out!"
The porter stood watching him and didn't move.
"Jesus," Haze said. "Jesus."
The porter didn't move. "Jesus been a long time gone," he said in a sour triumphant voice. (p. 27)

Here Miss O'Connor uses one of her favorite ironic techniques: in his blasphemous exclamations the character underscores the religious theme and reveals his hidden longings. Only Jesus *can* get Haze out of his coffin.

Yet at the same time that the dreams show a repressed longing for eternal life and for Jesus, who has saved man from death, they also show a conflicting fear of Jesus as his devourer, as symbolically the coffin that closes down to swallow up men. Even though the figures of his dreams fail, they try to escape from their coffins by their own wits and will power; they try to conquer death and Jesus by themselves so that they will have no need for redemption. In this sense, the dreams are metaphorical capsules of the main action of the novel, because Haze, like his nightmare alter-egos, will try futilely to outwit the "wild ragged figure" of Christ who moves in the back of his mind and summons him into the darkness. Paradoxically, then, for Haze, Jesus is both the deliverer from death and death itself. To be saved, man can gain his life only by losing it, and he must die to himself to be reborn as the "new man," as his true self. But Haze is possessed by Manichean, fundamentalist attitudes that prevent him from the full faith of Kierkegaard's knight; he sees his alternatives as the rejection of Christ or as complete self-destruction; he does not see salvation as a rebirth and a culmination of his essential being.

To escape Christ the devourer, whom he both desires and fears, Haze switches sides in his grandfather's Manicheism and begins to preach the reverse of the old man's religion. While in the army, Haze realizes, because he desperately wants to, that he would not need redemption if he had no soul, that he would not be sinful if there were no Fall and no such thing as sin, and that he could be peaceful and satisfied if Jesus were a liar. So he begins a religious crusade for the Church Without Christ, which is based on the single truth that there is no truth. Basically, he is preaching what everyone around him in the city believes, a relativistic, secular humanism. But they believe it quite comfortably, whereas he must violently and continuously assert his disbelief, because, like The Misfit, he is aware of the ultimate choices and must repeatedly deny Christ, just as the intense believer must repeatedly accept Him. Thus, Haze is an absurdity, an evangelistic atheist, a priest in the black mass of a humanistic religion that denies the validity of priests, masses, and religions. In cultural terms, he is just making explicit the demonic worship of man by those people who consider him a religious fanatic for expounding what they believe without realizing it. In psychological terms, he is trying to solve his dilemma by a simple inversion: by continuously renouncing a frightening and repressed desire, he can allow it to become conscious without accepting it. In religious terms, he is trying to maintain the demonic despair of defiance, to deify himself as the opponent of God ("Well I wouldn't [believe in Jesus] even if He existed. Even if He was on this train" [p. 16]).

Haze's ambivalent impulses toward and away from self-annihilation can be considered usefully in terms of Freud's concepts of *thanatos* and *eros*, for such an opposition helps to structure the central portion of the novel. Miss O'Connor did not accept Freud's quasi-biological interpretations of man, but she dealt with spiritual conflicts that can be approached in part from psychological theory, especially because the spiritual cannot be separated in her works from its various manifestations. In his later works Freud claimed that all organisms are impelled both toward self-preservation and more complex forms of development and toward simpler forms, toward an inert state possible only in death. This latter instinct shows the tendency of all organisms to shun the pain of unsatisfied desire and to seek equilibrium in rest. As an adjunct to this theory, Freud also came to believe that man is basically masochistic because he seeks self-destruction to fulfill the death instinct. To preserve the self, however, the life instinct turns self-destroying aggression outward toward other objects; it converts primal masochism into sadism.[3]

Insofar as Haze recoils from his desire for death in Christ, he, too, asserts the claims of life by turning his self-destructive impulses outward into aggression. And Miss O'Connor provides Haze with the two means that psychologists have discussed most often as man's attempts to escape death: sex and technology. When Haze first arrives in the city, he decides that he is going to do what people call sin to show that he does not believe in it, which merely shows how much he does believe in it since he is so compelled to prove that he does not,

Even before he starts preaching, he begins his crusade against death and Jesus by visiting a prostitute. As psychologists and theologians have often pointed out, concupiscent sexuality is almost never a matter of pleasure alone. It is the symbolic focus of many desires and fears in man's relation with others, himself, and God. Appropriately, Haze has no concern for sensuality in itself. Throughout the novel he is made embarrassed, indifferent, or frightened by the women who try to seduce him. Rather too patly, he intends to use the prostitute, Leora Watts, to assert the value of this world, of physical life, of *eros*. Since the time of Paul and Augustine, sexuality has been the main Christian symbol of concupiscence, and Haze is setting out to quiet his infinite longings with finite goods. An incident in his early childhood helped to establish the symbolic meanings of sexuality. Having gone with his father to a carnival and then having gotten into a "SINsational" sideshow, Haze looked down on a fat, naked woman who was lying, squirming, in a black-lined box. " 'Had one of them ther built into ever' casket,' his father, up toward the front, said, 'be a heap ready to go sooner' " (p. 62). After Haze got home, his mother, sensing his guilt, whipped him, saying, "Jesus died to redeem you." The next day he walked in the woods with his shoes filled with stones in penance. This incident, which Miss O'Connor juxtaposes with one of the visits to Mrs. Watts, is an overly explicit footnote to Haze's motives. The woman in the coffin, with the added comment by the father, opposes sexuality to death, and, with the mother's comments, she opposes it to Jesus and redemption. Furthermore, the incident makes a pat contrast between the lascivious woman and the stern, religious, prohibitive mother. In a sense, Haze is using Leora Watts not only to escape death but also to refute his religious mother by finding her replacement in a prostitute, a spiritless sexual object, a reduction of the other person to a thing. Although this psychological reading might seem too clinical for the book, Miss O'Connor several times points out a relation between the mother and the women

Haze meets. When he first visited Mrs. Watts and insisted that he was no preacher, "she put her other hand under his face and tickled it in a motherly way. 'That's okay, son,' she said. 'Momma don't mind if you ain't a preacher'" (p. 34). Later he is followed in the park by a mother with two children, who obviously wants to seduce him. And even Sabbath Lily Hawks, the young girl with whom he reluctantly makes love, is once represented as a parody of the Virgin Mother as she holds the mummified "new jesus" in her arms and says, "Call me Momma now" (p. 187). Naturally, Haze fails in all of his attempts at sexual aggressiveness. Mrs. Watts humors him, ridicules him, and finally cuts the top out of his preacher's hat for a joke; and, although he intends to seduce Sabbath Hawks to prove his disbelief to her preacher father, he ends up being seduced and quite obviously used by her.

Haze also tries to escape Jesus and death by buying himself a rat-colored, fifty-dollar car, which he uses as a house, a pulpit, and a means of trying to leave his failures. He has an intense, superstitious need for the old Essex, which recalls the car from which his grandfather preached, and he insists that "nobody with a good car needs to be justified" (p. 113). Miss O'Connor is again choosing a symbolic gesture that is central to Western culture. It has become a platitude in social and intellectual history that man often uses technology as a means to escape insecurity and the fear of death. It is a way to assert his control over nature and to convince himself that he is exempt from natural limitations. Machinery often has this significance in Miss O'Connor's stories (for instance, to Mr. Fortune in "A View of the Woods"), and in *Wise Blood* the car finally becomes the weapon with which Haze murders his impersonator, Solace Layfield. There are even some suggestions that Haze uses his car as an alternative to sexuality in his self-assertions, for the car is several times related to sex. When Haze is buying it, the salesman says to him, "We'll drive it around . . . or would you like to get under and look up it?" (p. 72); and when Sabbath Hawks tries to seduce him in the woods, he hurries back to his car, afraid that somebody might steal it. This association, too, is pat, for psychologists often consider the automobile to be a symbol of potency and aggressiveness for the emasculated man. Appropriately, Haze is no more successful as a driver than he is as a lover or an atheistic preacher. His car is finally pushed over an embankment by a policeman who decides that it is a public nuisance. (Incidentally, this polite, efficient, disinterested policeman is one of Miss O'Connor's best caricatures of man in collective, rationalistic society; he is G. B. Shaw's ideal of the pragmatic superman extended to its inhuman conclusion.)

By using a secondary character, Enoch Emery, whom a number of commentators have justifiably criticized as a serious fault in the structure of the book, Miss O'Connor includes one more basic form of man's self-assertion: romantic vitalism. Enoch feels that he has "wise blood," a kind of subrational bodily intuition inherited from his father. At times he is controlled by his unconscious impulses, which force him to do things he does not want to do but which he knows he must. The dark gods of his blood, in a likely parody of D. H. Lawrence's fiction, force him variously into awe, envy, and hatred of the animals in the zoo in which he works as a guard. He also worships a shrunken mummy in a museum (the "new jesus," who is "all man"), performs compulsive rituals, and appropriately ends up in a stolen gorilla suit, trying futilely to make friends with a frightened pair of lovers. The instinctualist can go no further than an apotheosis into an ape, and so he evaporates from the novel.

Hazel Motes, however, is not such a flat comic character, and he extends his assumed role through increasingly frenzied gestures until finally it collapses and he admits his longing for salvation. The climax comes in the highly symbolic scene in which Haze pursues and kills his impersonator, Solace Layfield, who has been dressing like Haze and trying to make money by preaching from his car about The Church of Christ

Without Christ, an ironic and revealing parody of Haze's Church Without Christ. As Haze runs over Layfield with his car, claiming that this prophet "ain't true," he kills his double and prepares for his own rebirth. The symbolic death of the double has become almost a convention in modern literature, and it would be a cheaply bought climax, except that Miss O'Connor has worked it so substantially into the themes and structure of the book that it is not merely a sign of the old self being put off for the new. Up to this point Haze has been a failure at violence in his attempts to turn his self-sacrificial impulses toward others. In each of his abortive efforts to be physically or verbally aggressive, he has ended up a victim, manipulated by the prostitutes, policeman, and hucksters who are more naturally sadistic than he is. Now, he succeeds at last in acting violently to defend his inverted faith, but he does so by symbolically killing himself. In murdering his double, he becomes both aggressor and victim, which in fact has been his dual role throughout. The murder is not only a turning point, but also a metaphorical explanation of what he has been doing in the entire novel. All of his self-assertions are futile, not only because he is trying to deceive himself, but because he wants basically to lose his self, his independence, to Jesus.

The murder is also a form of the comic sacrifice in "The Artificial Nigger." The pretender is unmasked, literally stripped of his preacher's clothing, and cast out to prepare for the rebirth of the hero. Once again, the overt action is an analogy for the psychological and spiritual conflict within the hero. Haze's new, although still embryonic, role as a believer is confirmed when he leans over the dying Layfield to hear the man's last words and shockingly finds himself hearing a confession. Thus, as a symbol of Haze, Layfield admits his guilt and desire for forgiveness; and, as himself, he turns the actual Haze into a priest.

After Haze has made a last, frenzied attempt to escape, only to have his justifying car destroyed by the policeman, he returns to his rooming house and begins his penance and his acceptance of Jesus. As Robert Fitzgerald has explained, Miss O'Connor "had reached an impasse with Haze and didn't know how to finish him off" until she read the Oedipus plays and decided to have him blind himself.[4] The blinded Haze also wraps his chest with barbed wire, puts gravel and broken glass in his shoes, throws away whatever money is left over from each government check, and retires into a nearly speechless calm. In part, he is performing a penance as extreme as his sin against the Holy Ghost, and he is expressing a faith as violent as his previous denial. But he is also fulfilling his persistent desire to surrender completely to the devouring Jesus, to sacrifice himself and be buried in the dark coffin.

I do not think that Miss O'Connor did entirely overcome her impasse, although she did make some admirable maneuvers. The main trouble was that she wanted a strong affirmation of Haze's rebirth, something more conclusive than the short stories that break off at the reversal, but the novel was not heading quite that way. For one thing, even when she used the *Oedipus Tyrannos* to suggest revelation and the acceptance of guilt, she had neither the space nor the character to write an *Oedipus Coloneus*, to show her hero as accepted, majestic, and justified. Still more importantly, she had to show Haze as finally accepting his religious impulses, which she had treated somewhat ambivalently in the early chapters of the novel. She had to show him seeking a spiritual consummation which, although infinitely better than the secular pottage offered him by other characters, is nevertheless tainted by Manicheism and morbidity. She had to do this because the whole symbolic and psychological structure of the novel offered two diametrically opposed alternatives to Haze, and there would have been no justification for his being suddenly enlightened in yet another possibility.

Trying to avoid this dilemma, Miss O'Connor performed some clever literary manipulations, although in doing so she threw the conclusion of the novel out of balance, as some critics have noted but without seeing why she did it. (I do not mean that she necessarily thought through these critical problems; she may just have responded to what she felt the book needed.) In the final chapter she shifted the center of attention to Mrs. Flood, Haze's landlady, who had scarcely been mentioned up to that point, and she presented Haze's religious phase either from Mrs. Flood's point of view or in direct contrast to the woman's attitudes. This technique has the obvious disadvantage of introducing a new important character at the last minute, and it makes the book seem more diffuse and anti-climactic. But it also makes Haze's religious attitudes seem completely admirable, since Mrs. Flood is a philistine who cannot understand why anyone would act the way her boarder does. She thinks that being "clean" is only a matter of hygiene and that if she were blind she would sit around all day, "eating cake and ice cream, and soaking her feet"; and she is shocked at his mortifications: " 'Well, it's not normal. It's like one of them gory stories, it's something that people have quit doing—like boiling in oil or being a saint or walling up cats,' she said. 'There's no reason for it. People have quit doing it' " (p. 224). Given such a comically inadequate point of view, the reader is not likely to be very critical of Haze's religious feelings; to question them at all would be in effect to side with Mrs. Flood, who thanks her stars every day that she is "not religious or morbid."

Furthermore, Miss O'Connor also gains the reader's assent by giving her philistine a blurred fragment of insight, which the reader completes and elaborates from his superior point of view. Mrs. Flood senses vaguely that Haze is aware of something she is not, that he has some reason for blinding himself, and that she is somehow being cheated out of something that he is wise to. She even feels that he sees something, and when she tries to imagine being blind, she thinks of a long dark tunnel with a pinpoint of light at the end, like the star on a Christmas card (pp. 218–19). In these last images of distant light Miss O'Connor has neatly and quietly transformed the images of darkness that Haze had associated with salvation in the opening chapters. *Mrs. Flood* introduces the idea of light in that darkness, which does not require that *Haze* has changed his conception but which does vaguely suggest that change. Thus, the reader is made to feel that Haze experiences the light of Christ's star, even though the author has not shown that kind of transformation, which the structure of the book would not justify. She gives the impression of the effects of grace indirectly, without having to show them in the character himself.

Such techniques are not really dishonest; they are part of the craftsman's right to manipulate his reader in order to achieve the effects he wants. And one should probably not demand theological consistency from a novel, even one that is concerned mainly with religious questions. But the book does have literary weaknesses that are related to an uncertain authorial point of view. Apart from some sociological triteness and a tendency at times to stuff in too much, Miss O'Connor falters in her authorial attitudes toward Haze's religious longings, since the attitudes seem to vary without any apparent change in Haze's basic longings themselves. Although there was much foolishness in early critical responses to *Wise Blood* that considered Haze to be a satirized fanatic, there is some justification for a reader's confusion about the way he is supposed to feel about Haze and his fundamentalism. There has been similar confusion over the Tarwaters' religion in *The Violent Bear It Away*, but I hope to show that it is not warranted, since that novel fully justifies the complex attitudes in it.

By the time Miss O'Connor wrote her second novel she had already published a collection of stories, and *The Violent Bear It Away* presented little trouble with point of view. Perhaps through the stories Miss O'Connor had worked out more fully the relation between natural and supernatural grace; perhaps she had clarified her attitudes toward the backwoods religion about which she wrote; and perhaps she had come to a fuller and more precise understanding of the ways in which men may both love and hate God. But whatever the cause, her second novel is precise and subtle in its main themes.

Several critics have disagreed and found the novel confused, but usually this has resulted from the critic's offering an inadequate interpretation and then criticizing the book for not always fitting it. This happens especially when the novel is schematized into a morality play. The fourteen-year-old protagonist, Francis Marian Tarwater, is seen as an allegorical Everyman who must choose between good and evil angels. The good angel is Mason Tarwater, the boy's great-uncle, a backwoods prophet who raises his nephew to be his successor and impresses upon him the central aim of a Christian, to be redeemed in Christ. The evil angel is the boy's uncle, George Rayber, the familiar rationalistic schoolteacher who tries to save the boy from superstition and suffering by helping him to renounce his religious upbringing. There is much validity to this scheme, since Miss O'Connor does stress the two men's competition for the boy, even to the extent of identifying them with the country and the city and having young Tarwater journey between them, much like the two travelers in "The Artificial Nigger." But the main difficulties with the scheme are that neither alternative is simple and that the progress of young Tarwater involves a great deal more than his finally choosing the right one.

No one seems to have much trouble with Rayber's complexity, since it is mostly psychological and does not complicate the reader's attitude toward him very much. Rayber is a compulsive rationalist who, himself, is trying desperately to overcome the effects that the old man had on him when he was seven years old. He is trying to become a complete philistine, to eliminate his irrational impulses, and to explain away his spiritual desires as madness instilled in him at an impressionable age. Since he is struggling to achieve emptiness, he is clearly not a flat symbol for rationalism or secular-

ism: he is a secondary protagonist undergoing a struggle similar to young Tarwater's, except that he is more advanced in
his renunciation of belief. These complexities make the character more interesting, more pathetic, even a little more sympathetic; he is not completely a comic fool, since he is aware
of the struggle and some of the issues. But they do not make
him or his way of life more admirable, for he is still a coward
and a self-deluding egoist. Obviously his way must be rejected
by young Tarwater. Although it is understandable, it is spiritually inadequate and ultimately self-defeating.

On the other side, many commentators do have trouble
with the assumed good angel of the morality play. As the
most obvious alternative to Rayber's desperate rationalism, old
Tarwater's religion creates almost as many problems for the
reader's peace of mind as it does for young Tarwater's. We
know that Miss O'Connor sees the old man as basically right
in his faith, not only because of the patterns of her other works
but also because the author has told us so: "Old Tarwater is
the hero of 'The Violent Bear It Away,' and I'm right behind
him 100 per cent." [5] Yet he is often petty, arrogant, vindictive,
and selfish; he is "a prophet with a still," making his living
selling stump liquor. At best, he is a fallen angel.

There have been two main ways of handling this violent
old man, either by blaming his faults on the age in which he
lives or by suggesting that the author is confused in her attitudes. The first approach is not adequate, because it merely
tries to avoid persistent problems in the book. It maintains
that a secular world has forced the true believer and prophet
into grotesquely extreme reactions against it. Since all other
men are reasonable, moderate infidels, the prophet seems—
and even becomes—a madman. So, old Tarwater's religion is
sound, but his manifestations of it are distorted by cultural
influences over which he has no control. Perhaps in the Middle Ages he would have been a saint instead of a partly comic,
partly destructive, largely correct fundamentalist. Commentators who have not been satisfied with this interpretation have

tended to oversimplify the character in an opposite manner, emphasizing the old man's distortions of Christianity. Irving Malin has pointed out the narcissism in that "church of self-love" and has suggested that old Tarwater saw his own distorted image in the biblical prophets he imitated. Similarly, Louis Rubin has emphasized old Tarwater's hatred and his devotion to a God of Wrath as opposed to the God of Love described by the child-evangelist.[6] These observations do point out legitimate problems in the novel, but they do not end in solutions since they substitute one partial conception of the character for another. At best, they lead to Rubin's claim that Miss O'Connor probably did not intend the critique of fundamentalism and the schism she created between a god of wrath and a god of love.

I believe that Miss O'Connor did intend that critique and that schism, for she worked it in great detail into the structure of her novel and the conception of all three of the main characters. Furthermore, the problem is not unique to this work, but appears in her stories and in *Wise Blood*. To see what Miss O'Connor has done with old Tarwater is to see that the novel is not confused but carefully patterned, and it is also to see how her Christian humanism culminates in her most ambitious work. In this second novel she overcomes most of the weaknesses of her first and brings into sharp focus the central concerns of all of her work.

The old man is not merely a symbol of faith or an example of narcissism; he is a complex character who, like all men, must struggle continuously to cast out the old Adam. In one sense, he is the hero of the novel because he is in travail and, despite his repeated lapses, triumphs over himself, not once but many times. He is basically a good and faithful man, but since "in us the good is something under construction," goodness can never be a simple possession for man: it is constantly being constructed, and the work is often undone. So, when Miss O'Connor says that she is "behind him 100 per cent," she may well be backing him in a struggle with himself as with unbelievers. And this struggle is more basic than that of a holy man with the weaknesses of the flesh, for it concerns old Tarwater's relation to God, to other men, and to himself— that is, the whole range of Christian relationships involved in the problem of man's wholeness and estrangement. It is centered in the conflict that has reappeared in various forms throughout this study, the conflict between selfhood and selflessness which Christian humanism requires must be resolved.

As one might expect from Miss O'Connor's other works, old Tarwater fails repeatedly through an excess of egoism, and he is repeatedly corrected by a destruction of that proud self. What may have obscured this conflict for most readers is that it does not take one of the forms most common in Miss O'Connor's stories or in *Wise Blood*: it does not oppose rationalism, defiance, or complacency to faith. Instead, it deals with opposing attitudes of religious belief in one of the intensely faithful, with a man who is at different times a false prophet and a true prophet, depending upon the relationship between selfhood and selflessness within the belief. The old man was a powerful and sometimes violent prophet of Jesus, but at times he saw his vocation from the self-righteous position of the elect, and he saw himself as the scourge of God, vengefully commanding punishment on all who would not listen to him:

> He had been called in his early youth and had set out for the city to proclaim the destruction awaiting a world that had abandoned its Saviour. He proclaimed from the midst of his fury that the world would see the sun burst in blood and fire and while he raged and waited, it rose every morning, calm and contained in itself, as if not only the world, but the Lord Himself had failed to hear the prophet's message.[7]

From what is disclosed of the city throughout the novel, the old man had a certain point: the world had abandoned its savior, and it did seem well on the way to destroying itself one way or another. But his use of God to justify his own hatred and his assumption of omnipotence shows that he has much in common with Mrs. Shortley, the false prophet of "The Displaced Person," who felt herself called to prophesy that the children of wicked nations would be butchered. Like Mrs. Shortley, he violated the role of the true prophet by separating himself from his people and ignoring his own uncleanliness. He overlooked what he could have learned from Micah or Isaiah or Jeremiah, that the chosen people of Israel were subject to pride in their election and were themselves the special object of chastisement.

To some extent the old man's fury and self-righteousness justified the comment made about him by young Tarwater's stranger, the interior devil, when he said, "That's all a prophet is good for—to admit somebody else is an ass or a whore" (p. 40). The devil was using the old man's weakness to scorn all prophecy, but he was still using a valid insight into old Tarwater's confused motives. Rayber did much the same thing when he denounced his uncle's calling in clinical statements so obviously inadequate that their partial truth may be overlooked. He wrote in an article for a schoolteachers' magazine, " 'His fixation of being called by the Lord had its origin in insecurity. He needed the assurance of a call, and so he called himself' " (p. 19). Although Rayber was trying to explain away in easy psychological terms the calling that he, too, was trying to resist, he understood correctly one of the motives of his uncle's dedication. This explanation is not only a truism of clinical psychology, it seems ironically fundamental in the religious psychology of the demonic. Kierkegaard claims that dread, anxiety, or "insecurity" is behind all attempts to escape from man's ambiguous nature, including the escape into self-justification and righteousness. Old Tarwater sensed that there was some truth to the explanation of his calling, although he could not admit it to himself. He was obsessed with the accusation, and when later recounting his life story, he would dwell on these statements with an anger that would leave him hissing in denial: " 'Called myself. I called myself.

I, Mason Tarwater, called myself! Called myself to be beaten and tied up. Called myself to be spit on and snickered at. Called myself to be struck down in my pride. Called myself to be torn by the Lord's eye. Listen boy . . . , even the mercy of the Lord burns' " (p. 20). The irony here is still more complex than in Miss O'Connor's use of the devil or the self-deceived rationalist to impart religious insights. In this passage old Tarwater had acknowledged and rejected the pride of his youth, and he had accepted the penance given him by the Lord. In fact, his last statement, "even the mercy of the Lord burns," has often and quite justly been cited as one of the central themes of the novel. Nevertheless, as T. S. Eliot has sugested in *Murder in the Cathedral,* there can be pride in martyrdom, and Miss O'Connor knew that a man could use his whippings to assure himself of his election. The old man's hatred in denouncing Rayber indicated that the charge touched a sensitive spot, and the hatred, itself, was a sign of pride and a sign that the mercy of the Lord had not burned him completely clean.

The pride of the false prophet also helped to form his attitude toward his great-nephew, creating a relationship in some way similar to that between Mr. Head and his grandson in "The Artificial Nigger" or between Mr. Fortune and his granddaughter in "A View of The Woods." Each of these old men considered himself the only suitable guide for the young person; each saw his own image reflected in the child; each attempted to mold the child into a closer likeness of himself; each engaged the child in a continuous and often comic competition. For Mason Tarwater this competition usually centered on the vocation of the prophet as he attempted to show that he truly had been called and was thoroughly qualified to instruct. Finally, the old man's pride was shown in his preoccupation with his burial, the burden of which he placed on the boy. His concern for last things is not entirely satirized, but the egoism in his concern for personal salvation often is. As in the description that Faulkner uses for the religious Cora

Tull in *As I Lay Dying,* Tarwater seemed as though he was "trying to crowd other folks away and get in closer than anybody else." The ambiguity in old Tarwater's concern for a proper burial is captured repeatedly in Miss O'Connor's complex style, which moves from the mystery of one's death in Christ (" 'The world was made for the dead. Think of all the dead there are. . . .' ") to broad graveyard comedy (" 'I ain't going to die in bed,' the old man said. 'As soon as I hear the summons, I'm going to run downstairs. I'll get as close to the door as I can.' " [pp. 16, 14]).

Yet Mason Tarwater's pride in his calling, suffering, mentorship, and salvation does not fully describe his nature, for he is not just a comic character. During his lifetime he had several religious experiences in which there was no pride or egoism, experiences that indicate the nature of Miss O'Connor's true prophet and provide a standard by which the rest of his life can be judged. The first incident occurred when, as a young man, he had gone forth to preach the coming destruction of the world. The fire had descended on him instead: "His own blood had been burned dry and not the blood of the world" (p. 6). Later, when he had come to take his great-nephew away from Rayber, "his range of vision had been clear. He had known what he was saving the boy from and it was saving and not destruction he was seeking. He had learned enough to hate the destruction that had to come and not all that was going to be destroyed" (p. 6). What old Tarwater had learned is vitally important for the prophet, for it is fundamental to Christianity even though it was sometimes obscured in Judaic prophecy: divine justice is infused with divine mercy; sins are forgiven but without abolishing the distinction between goodness and evil; and all men are too guilty to desire the destruction of the sinful.

As some of Miss O'Connor's short stories indicate, even a purification by fire does not cleanse man once and for all; if one birth is not enough for man, neither are two. Since old Tarwater was still able to protect his pride by becoming the boy's instructor and finding assurance in his own self-righteous sacrifices, he repeatedly had to be purified by God's mercy. So, there were moments when his confidence would weaken. At times while recounting his history he would realize that he had not only failed to rescue Rayber from atheism but had helped to drive him to rebellion against God:

> He would stop telling the story to Tarwater, stop and stare in front of him as if he were looking into a pit which had opened up before his feet.
>
> At such times he would wander into the woods and leave Tarwater alone in the clearing, occasionally for days, while he thrashed out his peace with the Lord, and when he returned, bedraggled and hungry, he would look the way the boy thought a prophet ought to look. He would look as if he had been wrestling a wildcat, as if his head were still full of the visions he had seen in its eyes, wheels of light and strange beasts with giant wings of fire and four heads turned to the four points of the universe. (p. 8)

Appropriately, he would seem most a prophet when most humbled, as if he were capable of visionary experiences only after he had looked into a pit of his own despair and inadequacy. The balance of these qualities is perfectly right for the true prophet created by a Christian humanist, for it suggests the restored balance between the egocentric and ecstatic forces of agape. And, at his best, the old man suggests this balance, this wholeness. He is certainly far from a mystic; even his preoccupation with death has an earthy robustness that suggests Chaucer more than St. John of the Cross (" 'This is the end of us all,' the old man said with satisfaction, his gravel voice hearty in the coffin" [p. 14]), and the use of the multiplied loaves and fishes to represent salvation is quite appropriate to the fat old man whose stomach rose above the top of the coffin like "over-leavened bread," an image which suggests both his earthiness and his real desire for the bread of life. However, his essential self was most fully completed when he admitted his dependency and weakness and did not assert claims against God. In such dependency he was completed, not destroyed. He ceased for the moment to be a comic character, pulled by conflicting impulses, and became a more centered character, even with a rude, awesome dignity. He became a true prophet, elevated in character and spirit when cast down.

In her complex handling of old Tarwater, Miss O'Connor avoided the ambiguities of her first novel. Hazel Motes began by inadequately thinking of salvation as a complete destruction of his self—as drowning and being eaten—and he opposed this with a grotesque self-assertion. Miss O'Connor then had difficulty bringing him to a more adequate understanding of salvation, in terms of Christian humanism. Old Tarwater, however, understood that salvation was fulfillment though destruction of the sinful self. He came to understand this when he first went forth to prophesy destruction and the fire descended on him. So, instead of fearing drowning as Haze did, he considered water to be baptismal; he saw it as generative as well as destructive, as the means of rebirth through death. Instead of imagining salvation as being eaten by a "soul-hungry Jesus," he saw it as being fed and nourished with the bread of life. This scriptural image, which pervades the novel, is a perfect symbol for the Christian humanist. In John 6:48–59 Jesus describes himself as the bread of life, which He then extends into the promise of the Eucharist: "If any man eat of this bread, he shall live forever; and the bread that I will give, is my flesh, for the life of the world." The bread of life symbolizes the Incarnation, the Word made flesh, and it promises the resurrection of the faithful. It reconciles the two realms that Manicheism separates. Since old Tarwater had such a valid conception of faith and salvation, he did not swing between two extremes of Gnosticism and atheism. He did lapse from true prophecy through pride and insecurity and thus lost the Christian balance of selfhood and selflessness by assuming righteousness and the right of judgment. But he was also capable of being restored by the mercy of God and by the very insecurity that caused him to become self-righteous.

I dwell on this character who dies in the early chapters of the book because he has been oversimplified in previous interpretations, but also because one must understand his complex attitudes to understand fully the other two major characters. In the first of the three sections of the novel, the old man's great-nephew, Francis Tarwater, shows a mixture of religious attitudes similar to his great-uncle's. One cannot fully understand the boy's rebellion against his vocation or his final acceptance of it until one sees that the boy, like his great-uncle, had conflicting conceptions of that vocation.

Commentators have overlooked the fact that young Tarwater was not initially opposed to becoming a prophet, providing that the role was sufficiently awe-inspiring. When he would see his great-uncle emerging from the woods, looking as though he had seen the wheels of light and strange beasts of apocalyptic scripture, the boy "knew that when he was called he would say, 'Here I am, Lord, ready!'" (p. 8). Although he scorned baptizing his idiot cousin, he did not scorn all missions that the Lord might send: "'He don't mean for me to finish up your leavings. He has other things in mind for me.' And he thought of Moses who struck water from a rock, of Joshua who made the sun stand still, of Daniel who stared down lions in the pit" (pp. 9–10). Believing that God had special plans for him, young Tarwater would walk in the woods, futilely waiting for a bush to flame up as a sign. With much of his great-uncle's egotism the boy was understandably attracted to the powers of Old Testament prophets. A faith that can summon up such miraculous proofs is reassuring; it testifies to one's strength, to one's control of the world and even of dark powers beyond the world. It satisfies one's pride and aggressiveness. But it is a form of the demonic, a form of the superstition which Miss O'Connor had satirized in "The River," in which the believers come to be healed in the muddy river and to see their preacher perform miracles even though he disclaims such egotistical power.

The role and the reward of the Christian prophet are not nearly so spectacular. If one renounces the world, one receives in exchange only the bread of life: "Had the bush flamed for Moses, the sun stood still for Joshua, the lions turned aside before Daniel only to prophesy the bread of life? Jesus? He felt a terrible disappointment in that conclusion, a dread that it was true" (p. 21). Young Tarwater also feared the terrible insufficiency he would feel as the prophet of Jesus. With the bottom split out of his stomach he would hunger continuously for something that the world could not adequately provide. Perhaps most importantly, he would have to sacrifice his independence, his proud separateness. The freedom he would achieve would paradoxically depend on Jesus, not solely on his own will. The world, in relation to which he could try to define himself, would become mysterious and evade all categories in which he might try to fix it; and in the context of infinity the individual self would seem to be nothing. When the demonic voice in his head told him that his choice "ain't Jesus or the devil. It's Jesus or *you*," this voice of the devil and his unconscious desires was not completely wrong. It was insidiously lying when it denied the existence of the devil and opposed Jesus to one's essential self, but it was right in making explicit the basic conflict within young Tarwater, the conflict between fulfillment in Jesus and the apparent self-sufficiency of estrangement, which is actually the choice of the devil. Until the climax of the novel, however, Tarwater did not understand clearly his alternatives, largely because he did not fully understand the meaning of salvation and of Christian prophecy. Somewhat like Hazel Motes, he feared salvation as complete self-destruction, and he set out to escape it by an aggressive defiance and self-assertion. But in *The Violent Bear It Away* the climactic revelations have been well prepared, both through the religion of old Tarwater and through the partial insights that young Tarwater has from the beginning of the novel. The main progression of the book is the preparation of the boy to accept and, above all, to understand more fully the meaning of the Christian prophet and of salvation.

After the old man had died, the boy went off to the city to find out the truth about things and to escape the prophetic vocation that had been passed on to him. He went to live with his uncle, Rayber, consciously because the schoolteacher offered an alternative to old Tarwater's life and unconsciously because Rayber's idiot son, Bishop, was the object of the prophetic task set by the old man. When the boy arrived at the uncle's house, he confronted the idiot child and received his calling:

> Then the revelation came, silent, implacable, direct as a bullet. He did not look into the eyes of any fiery beast or see a burning bush. He only knew, with a certainty sunk in despair, that he was expected to baptize the child he saw and begin the life his great-uncle had prepared him for. He knew that he was called to be a prophet and that the ways of his prophecy would not be remarkable. His black pupils, glassy and still, reflected depth on depth his own stricken image of himself, trudging into the distance in the bleeding stinking mad shadow of Jesus, until at last he received his reward, a broken fish, a multiplied loaf. (p. 91)

In trying to resist this call to Jesus, Tarwater showed the same qualities he had associated with his distorted conception of Old Testament prophets, violence and proud independence, although throughout Part II of the novel he often showed the qualities merely through sullenness and petty bickerings with his uncle. In his carpings at Rayber and in his weak attempts to ignore the idiot, Bishop, he tried for awhile to avoid the whole issue of his calling, to ease out of his dilemma by keeping his eyes fixed on the surface of things. But, like the bourgeoise farmwomen of the stories, he could not entirely anesthetize himself in the trivial. Through violently disrupting experiences he was called back to the task of baptizing Bishop. As he became more openly obsessed with the idiot-child, he realized that he could not rid himself of his calling by merely not beginning it. He could not imitate Rayber, the dedicatedly lukewarm, who, unable to accept or reject Jesus, tried desperately to remain inactive and empty, who was proud that he could force himself not to act (which is a rationalization after the fact). But Tarwater came to realize that Jesus had thrown everything off balance and that one who knew this fully could not sit poised at the still center. Like The Misfit, he realized that you had to throw everything away and follow Jesus or you had to do some meanness to somebody. He felt, as Reverend Bevel Summers in "The River" commanded, that you had to testify to Jesus or the devil. As the plot reaches its climax in the last chapter of Part II, Tarwater had decided that "you can't just say No. . . . You got to do NO." The issue had become absolutely defined and uncompromisable; no amount of self-justifying talk could obscure his radical choice of doing No or doing YES. So, asserting his allegiances, he took Bishop out onto the lake surrounded by the dark symbolic woods and drowned him.

But often in Miss O'Connor's works actions tend to suggest their opposites, for YES and NO—as opposite as they most surely are—have more in common with each other than with the gray middle of emptiness. As Tarwater drowns Bishop, he involuntarily baptizes him, which is a fine narrative and thematic touch that bothers many readers who worry about free will in the novel. Yet, the double action is psychologically and spiritually right. Both The Misfit and Hazel Motes had expressed their denials of Jesus through murder, and both had thus expressed their intense belief in the God they had to deny. (Human nature being what it is, one must also admit the inverse: "Lord, I believe; help thou mine unbelief.") Like these other two characters, Tarwater could not settle his conflict once and for all by an act of denial: the murder-baptism (simultaneously doing NO and doing YES) shows how ambiguous such a desperate act must be. As long as the conflict remains strong, as long as man is a spiritually vital being, no act of denial can be conclusive. This is true to a lesser extent of affirmations, although God's grace further completes those acts. The devil, however, has no grace to give.

Furthermore, the involuntary baptizing does not show that Tarwater was theologically or psychologically predestined; it shows rather that his spiritual conflict could not be solved so easily, and perhaps that it could never be entirely resolved in man's mortal and fallen state. Readers who stress predestination often seem to think that the novel has more or less stopped developing at this point, that Part III is an epilog explaining what had already taken place through the baptism. But this is not so at all. The turning point had occurred in the fortunes of Tarwater, the heroic antagonist; but the struggle went on, and the discovery—with the growth of Tarwater, the spiritual protagonist—lay ahead. The narrative pattern here is similar to that of "Revelation": Mrs. Turpin suffered a climactic defeat in the doctor's office, but she still struggled to deny the implications of the defeat until her travail brought her to a revelation and an admission. In the terms of traditional dramatic structure, these two tragi-comic heroes suffered a reversal at their height of frantic self-assertion. Although they struggled to resist their declining emotional fortunes, they ended in a catastrophic destruction of their pride. This tragic pattern, however, is complemented by a pattern of Christian comedy, since the defeat of the proud and independent hero generated the birth of his spiritual, dependent self. This double pattern of comic birth out of tragic defeat is central to almost all of Miss O'Connor's work, both to her main themes and her narrative structures.

Appropriately, Tarwater increasingly progressed from the aggressive murderer to the passive victim, even while he tried futilely to assert himself and his independence. Although Bishop was not Tarwater's double (as Solace Layfield was Hazel Motes's), the murder has suggestions of a symbolic suicide, as is underscored by a biblical allusion. As the sleeping Tarwater relived the murder through a nightmare, he flailed about and was associated with an Old Testament prophet.

But this time the association was not with Moses, Joshua, or Daniel: "His pale face twitched and grimaced. He might have been Jonah clinging wildly to the whale's tongue" (p. 216). The archetypal and theologically antetypal image describes the reversal: in drowning Bishop, Tarwater had begun to reenact symbolically the death and resurrection of Jonah and Christ.

Throughout the rest of his journey to defeat and salvation he was further humiliated in a series of increasingly violent assaults on his pride. First, a truck driver, who needed company at night to stay awake, ridiculed him and finally told him to get out of the truck: " 'I don't ride nuts in the day time.' " While still in the truck, Tarwater had found in his hat a business card given him by T. Fawcett Meeks, the salesman who had originally driven him to town. Meeks, as his name ironically suggests, was an ingratiating man of calculated friendliness. He had tried to befriend the boy to get a cheap, hardworking assistant. This reference to Meeks underscores the difference between Tarwater's two journeys. Although the truck driver was also trying to use the boy, he was hardly meek or insidious in his manner. His harsh, cynical directness was reflected in his truck, which grated away like a "gigantic monster." In this return journey, in the falling action of the novel, the commercial exploiters had become more brutal, and the hero was scorned rather than humored. Next he was judged by a storeowner who knew of his blasphemy. This woman, too, has her parallel in the first part of the novel, in the Negroes who scolded Tarwater for shirking his burial duty; and again the parallel emphasizes the difference in the boy's state. Unlike the Negroes, she was not tactful and easy in her reprimand but was stern and even awesome. Here too, the imagery suggests the change of experience: "There was all knowledge in her stony face and the fold of her arms indicated a judgment fixed from the foundations of time. Huge wings might have been folded behind her without seeming strange" (p. 225). Finally, in the third encounter the increasing violence and symbolism becomes almost surreal. Tarwater was drugged and raped by a satanic, vampiric homosexual, wearing a lavender shirt and panama hat. Clearly this character is an incarnation and gothic extension of Tarwater's "stranger," the interior voice that began, after the great-uncle's death, to tempt him into self-concern and self-indulgence.

Several commentators have objected to the rape as unnecessary sensationalism, but it is quite functional. Not only does it complete the parallels with the first journey, but it also pushes the humiliation of this self-righteously ascetic boy into self-disgust. Furthermore, the gothic extremity of the scene fits the developing tone and imagery of the journey. As Tarwater neared Powderhead, as he was progressively humbled and victimized, his surroundings were transformed. He was entering another country, a spiritual landscape which reflected his increasing desperation, his increasing susceptability to revelation, and—more objectively—the religious issues involved. His surroundings had become nearly apocalyptic, with the ground seeming like "the back of a giant beast which might any moment stretch a muscle and send him rolling into the ditch below" and with a wooden bridge like "the skeleton of some prehistoric beast" (pp. 220, 233). He was traveling farther from Rayber's balanced, rational, spiritually empty world and was moving into a radically different world in which all objects and incidents were transformed by spiritual values. Like Mr. Head and Nelson in "The Artificial Nigger," he had to descend into the demonic world, to feel terror, humiliation, and guilt, before he could experience his revelation and begin to be reborn. He had to confront the devil and to realize that the self he had tried to assert against Jesus was of the devil's party. Finally, as he arrived home in despair, he discovered that even his first act of defiance, his cremation of the great-uncle, had been a failure, since a Negro neighbor had buried the old man before the boy woke from his drunken sleep and set fire to the house.

Defeated in his rebellion, he at last admitted his hunger for the bread of life, a hunger that he felt "building from the blood of Abel," the first victim. As with O. E. Parker in "Parker's Back," the hunger had always been in him, unadmitted, gnawing, forcing him to realize that he could never satisfy it with worldly possessions, no matter how much they flattered him. He realized that the bread of life, although worthless in terms of the world's vanity, was the only possession for which he longed and that it must be received as a gift. Then, in the fire he had set as a last violent protest against the evil that had raped him and the darkness that was enveloping him, he saw his sign:

> He knew that this was the fire that had encircled Daniel, that had raised Elijah from the earth, that had spoken to Moses and would in the instant speak to him. He threw himself to the ground and with his face against the dirt of the grave, heard to command, GO WARN THE CHILDREN OF GOD OF THE TERRIBLE SPEED OF MERCY. The words were as silent as seeds opening one at a time in his blood. (p. 242)

Although several critics, pointing out recurring symbols, have noted that there are many earlier references to fire and prophets, there has been a general disregard for the changed significance of these symbols. The fiery sign did not come as the burning bush Tarwater once expected to confirm his majesty and power; it came as the "red-gold tree of fire," Christ's rood-tree, to singe his eyes and consume his old self in God's burning mercy. At this time he also realized that even the Old Testament prophets had had to bear their miracles as burdens and that even their glory had come not from their power but from their submission to the power of God. The irony of these coalescing images points to a central irony in the messianic tradition: that the Messiah, the King, came to sacrifice himself for his people, and in doing so he showed that man's grandeur came in the humility of self-sacrifice. Thus, Tarwater did not merely yield to a calling he had always understood; he came to understand more fully the nature of all true prophets, to understand the relationship of glory and abasement. Like his great-uncle before him, he realized at last that the Lord

131

raises only those whom He has thrown down and that even such elevation is not compatible with pride. Old Tarwater, himself, had emphasized this change in understanding when he had said to the insolent boy, "the day may come . . . when a pit opens up inside you and you know some things you never known before" (p. 67). Such a change of consciousness, like the epiphanies throughout Miss O'Connor's works, is not simply received but also attained as an act of free will. It is a creative, volitional act of perception that is appropriate to the character, his experiences, and his circumstances but that is not determined by them. The commentators who have claimed that Tarwater lacks freedom in accepting his calling have seen him as a fairly static character who finally stops fighting and gives in to his fate. They neglect to see that a series of revelations, made possible by the boy's experiences, makes him able to accept that calling. And such revelations, more than any action resulting from them, are the main achievements of many of Miss O'Connor's characters. In her stories, grace is most often enlightenment, especially about oneself; and as I have tried to show throughout, it is the fulfillment of a character's nature.

As Tarwater accepts and begins his mission, several details play ironically on earlier passages about prophecy and thereby emphasize the change in the boy's conceptions. When he had first gone to the city with his great-uncle, he looked down at the streets from an office window and thought that "when he was called, on that day when he returned, he would set the city astir, he would return with fire in his eyes" (p. 28). Immediately there was an ironic foreshadowing as his hat (a symbol of identity and aggressiveness for many of her characters, as well as for Freud's dreamers) fell off his head and floated down "to be smashed in the tin river below." The irony is fulfilled in the conclusion of the book, when he returns to prophesy, not with fire in his eyes, but with "his singed eyes, black in their deep sockets." There is also irony in the command that comes to the boy. Once when the great-uncle had gone to his sister's house to shout on her doorstep, filled with righteous indignation at the sinner, he had cried out, " 'The Lord is preparing a prophet with fire in his hand and eye and the prophet is moving toward the city with his warning. The prophet is coming with the Lord's message. 'Go warn the children of God,' saith the Lord, 'of the terrible speed of justice.' Who will be left? Who will be left when the Lord's mercy strikes?' " (p. 60). The last questions echo the prophecy of Mrs. Shortley, the vindictive false prophet of "The Displaced Person" (" 'Who will remain whole? Who?' "), and as in that story, it emphasizes that none will be left untouched, including the self-righteous prophets. The preceding part of the old man's prophecy is even more pointedly related to young Tarwater's calling. The boy did become the prophet prepared by the Lord, but a prophet who was burned rather than one who burned. Moreover, the command the boy received differed importantly from that predicted by the old man: "the terrible speed of justice" is replaced by "the terrible speed of mercy." The shift of emphasis in the message suggests that "even the mercy of the Lord burns," as the boy would learn in his own purification. But, more importantly, it suggests that the prophet of wrath and destruction was replaced by the prophet of mercy and salvation. So, his forehead smeared with dust of mortality from the grave and his eyes singed by fire as were the lips of Isaiah, the Christian prophet went forth to warn the children of God to prepare but also to preach the forgiveness of sin, perhaps realizing that none will be left unburnt.

In the conclusion of the novel, Tarwater had lost much of his individuality, at least that which had come from estrangement, and we are fearfully aware that he would never be one of the comfortable and familiar people of the earth. But when we try to determine exactly what had been lost in terms of the actual character and not in terms of irrelevant concepts of identity, we must not exaggerate the worth of what Tarwater had lost: a comic arrogance, petulance, anxiety, anger, egoism, and perhaps something of a sarcastic wit. To value these qualities more than Tarwater's transformation is modern sentimentalism, like wishing that Milton's Satan had won the heavenly battle because he was wittier and more energetic than Milton's God or like objecting to Shakespeare's Henry V because he could not remain Prince Hal. Individuality, in the sense of uniqueness, is nearly as unimportant an end of human existence as conformity, for both ends are complementary solutions to the same trivial questions about man's nature. Moreover, Tarwater had hardly been immolated. The final image of him implies power, will, firmness, even the ability at last to commit a centered act that is not made futile by conflicting motives. He had the disturbing calmness of certainty. Some readers, in fact, have considered him a terrifying madman and fanatic as he went off toward the defenseless children of God, an extreme response which sacrifices the whole structure of the novel for a few isolated images but which does recognize his violent prophetic power.

Tarwater does not represent an ideal of Christian humanism, but then the prophet never does, for he comes to correct a sinful world and he is restricted by the intense focus of his mission. Tarwater was isolated from the rest of mankind and unable to feel the goodness of the natural world, but prophets are not gregarious and the world does not lack appreciators. He had balanced his longing for prophetic grandeur and his longing for Jesus and the bread of life; he had even achieved much of the Christian humanist's balance between the power of egoism and the selflessness of sacrifice. The balance was perhaps precarious and could not become the more stable resolution of, say, Father Flynn of "The Displaced Person." It was instead a conjunction of violent opposites, as the last paragraph of the novel suggests in its imagery:

By midnight he had left the road and the burning wood behind him and had come out on the highway once more. The moon, riding low above the field beside him, appeared and disappeared, diamond-bright, between patches of darkness. Intermittently the boy's jagged shadow slanted across the road ahead of him as if it cleared a rough path toward his goal. His singed eyes, black in their deep sockets, seemed already to envision the fate that awaited him but he moved steadily on, his face set toward the dark city, where the children of God lay sleeping. (p. 243)

The diamond-brightness alternating with darkness, the rough path superimposed on the more definite highway, the jagged shadow, singed eyes, and acceptance of fate contrasted with the steady movement, set face, and sense of a goal—these opposites reflect the contraries within Tarwater, and we should not slight the violence and terror that this prophet was bringing to the sleeping children of God. But Tarwater was no rough beast, slouching toward an ironically inverted second coming; in the terms that Miss O'Connor had used for the great-uncle, "it was saving and not destruction he was seeking. He had learned enough to hate the destruction that had to come and not all that was going to be destroyed" (p. 6). The destruction did have to come and Tarwater was to be its instrument. The image of sleeping children should make us feel pity and fear for them, but it should also remind us that they had to be awakened. And this boy (for the last lines remind us that he too was a child), this boy who had been destroyed and awakened, had now to awaken them through the power and humility of the Christian prophet.

In discussing Tarwater's development I have concentrated on the first and third parts of the novel, for the second part is essentially an intensification of Tarwater's conflict at the end of Part I. As other commentators have noted, the novel (like *Wise Blood*) is weakest in its middle, for there the main plot of Tarwater's struggle, defeat, and victory is largely biding time. The boy becomes more desperate and more aware that he cannot escape into Rayber's bland world, but these changes do not much complicate or broaden his dilemma. The cause of this structural problem seems fairly obvious. In the architecturally sound stories Miss O'Connor moves quickly from exposition to violent climax and reversal, but when she uses this short-story pattern in her novels, she weakens the effect by prolonging her opening exposition into a central mock-complication.

In both novels she tries to flesh out the center sections by means of subplots. In *Wise Blood* she uses Enoch Emery to parallel and caricature Haze's efforts to become a natural, godless man. In *The Violent Bear It Away* she develops Rayber as a secondary protagonist, which somewhat confuses his role in the book. As he participates directly in the main plot, Rayber represents the profane rationalism that Tarwater must not only reject but also outgrow as he passes into a very different order of existence. Consequently, Rayber (like Enoch Emery) disappears from the novel when it reaches its climax. But as Rayber is the protagonist of the subplot, he, too, struggles and even reaches something of revelation about himself.[8] Miss O'Connor does achieve a thematic unity of the two plots by making Rayber's conflict parallel those of the Tarwaters, although, of course, the conclusion of his struggle is the inverse of theirs.

Like the Tarwaters, Rayber was pulled in opposite directions by egoism and self-sacrifice. In the first place, he, too, was obsessed with selfhood and independence. Repeatedly he stressed human dignity, his will, and his power to choose emptiness over a rebirth that would cause insatiable longings. He saw himself as capable of a tragic gesture of renunciation, but in his last scene in the novel he was condemned in his own terms, for he realized that he no longer had the ability to choose—he had become empty. Having listened to the cries of his drowning idiot son, "he stood waiting for the raging pain, the intolerable hurt that was his due, to begin, so that he could ignore it, but he continued to feel nothing" (p. 203). The satiric ironies here, intensified by the rhythm of the sentence and of Rayber's thoughts, judge him as effectively as anything in the novel. In the second place, Rayber, like old Tarwater, saw himself as the only suitable mentor for his nephew. He regarded young Tarwater as an object to be possessed (" 'Now you belong to someone who can help you and understand you' ") and as a disciple to be properly molded ("he gazed through the actual insignificant boy before him to an image of him that he held fully developed in his mind" [p. 90]). To the extent that both of the boy's instructors were less concerned with him than with their own roles as prophet or schoolteacher, they were egoistic. In fact, in this regard Rayber could be considered a false prophet of sociology and education.

Rayber's pride, however, was threatened by his uncontrollable experiences of self-destruction. Although he had almost succeeded in suppressing his desire for Jesus, he was at times overwhelmed by a senseless, "useless" love for his son. These ecstasies of love, which began with Bishop but soon extended to everything he hated, destroyed all of his self-sufficiency. Miss O'Connor describes these feelings as a "surge" and an "undertow," associating them with young Tarwater's symbolic drowning and baptism. Rayber also resembled Tarwater in trying to confine his struggle to Bishop so that he could better control it. Unlike his nephew, however, he had failed in his attempt to drown the idiot boy. Lacking the strength to commit a violently evil act, he lacked also the strength to be saved. As one of the lukewarm, caught between his desires to kill Bishop and to surrender to his love for the child, Rayber could do neither; he could only become empty.

The schoolteacher's self-possession was also disrupted by another child, Lucette, the evangelistic preacher at the revival meeting. Her sermon, which occurs almost exactly in the middle of the novel and was a late addition by Miss O'Connor,[9] is a choric commentary on the rest of the book. As Rayber listened helplessly outside a window of the temple, she preached that Jesus is love and that men must know what love is in order to recognize Jesus when he comes; thus she indirectly commented on Rayber's relationship with his son. Also, anticipating young Tarwater's final vision, she cried, " 'I've seen the

Lord in a tree of fire! The Word of God is a burning Word to burn you clean'" (p. 134). Both prophets' revelation is of Christ's flaming rood-tree, come to humble and save the faithful as well as the unfaithful. And, most importantly for the opposition of religious pride and self-abnegation, she scorned messianic hopes for a savior who was to come majestically to establish an earthly kingdom:

> God was angry with the world because it always wanted more. It wanted as much as God had and it didn't know what God had but it wanted it and more. . . . God told the world he was going to send it a king and the world waited. The world thought, a golden fleece will do for His bed. Silver and gold and peacock tails, a thousand suns in a peacock's tail will do for His sash. His mother will ride on a four-horned white beast and use the sunset for a cape. (pp. 130–31)

But the king had come as a blue-cold child, born to a plain winter-woman, and the world lamented that "love cuts like the cold wind and the will of God is plain as the winter" (p. 132). These contrasts between two conceptions of the Messiah, between two attitudes of the faithful concerning their claims on God, and between two forms of prophecy are inescapably relevant to the conflicts within each of the Tarwaters. Unlike Louis Rubin, I would not completely oppose Lucette's message to old Tarwater's fanaticism,[10] for part of that fanaticism was the violent self-surrender to Jesus that the girl commanded, while another part was the vanity she denounced. Unlike the Tarwaters, Raybcr was unable to resolve such a conflict, and outside the temple he was caught in a paralyzing dilemma similar to that he experienced with his son. Unable to give himself to the crippled child-preacher of love and unable to confront her with a final renunciation, he crouched on the ground and impotently turned off his hearing aid. As is often the case in Miss O'Connor's works, the man who is estranged from his essential self and cannot approach wholeness and equilibrium is unable to act; he is truly self-defeating in his spiritual and psychological anarchy.

This novel, like *Wise Blood* and most of the stories, is built upon parallel sets of opposites: a fear of Christ and a longing for Him, self-righteousness and the conviction of sin, hatred and love, aggression and self-destruction, pride and humility. Miss O'Connor believed that these opposites are inherent in human existence and that they need not be destructive as they are in Rayber. They may be integrated by a faith that recognizes God as the ground of man's essential self and of all existence. As she showed repeatedly, this integration is difficult and terrifying; it requires the violent balancing of forces that repeatedly threaten to destroy each other. Thus, man tries to escape his insufficiency, his dread, through demonic postures as various as his capacity for invention. But his postures cannot fully hide his anxiety or his infinite longing because they are basically at odds with reality; they are the protective sublimations of spiritual, psychological, and social neuroses. And, so, with God's burning mercy and under the weight of an insistent reality, those postures may suddenly fail, leaving man vulnerable and receptive, at a beginning, which he will have to renew moment by moment throughout his life. And from this possibility of continuous renewal comes the optimism of the Christian humanist, who believes not only that man can be saved for eternal life, but also that, through grace and the recognition of the spiritual bases of human life, man can be restored to his essential self and can then achieve fuller communion with all other men. Man would not cease to be mortal, and he would still await the final Revelation, but he would become fully, and truly, human.

Being honestly realistic about man's condition, Miss O'Connor did not try to represent this fully complex yet fully integrated state. Instead, she explored the ways in which men destroy it, and she implied some causes of this self-destructiveness. Because she combined the satirist's sharp eye for folly with the humanist's sense of complexity, she understood that men use varied and devious means to escape the responsibility of being human. In her characters these attempted escapes vary from religious smugness to militant atheism, from lechery to disgust with the flesh, from worship of social progress to longing for the past. And her analyses of the problems are not only various, but also important, as their resemblance to the works of major authors in other disciplines demonstrates. Although her range of settings and social groups is small, she is a significant chronicler of the human mind and spirit.

Furthermore, as a humanist, Miss O'Connor sensed that man's various problems were interconnected, that a serious distortion in one dimension of man's spiritual, psychological, and social nature would cause distortions in the other dimensions. And, as a devout Christian, she believed that the fundamental causes of these distortions were religious, centering on man's proper relation to God. She could therefore sustain an integral view of human life and describe the human comedy without despair or cynical amusement. She could achieve a balanced attitude that produced her finest literary qualities: satirical tough-mindedness combined with compassion, concern for transcendence tempered by delight in human gestures, and stylistic exuberance controlled by sureness of structure. These literary qualities, for which Miss O'Connor has often been praised, seem but the expression of her Christian humanism.

Notes

Preface

1. Josephine Hendin's *The World of Flannery O'Connor* (Bloomington: Indiana University Press, 1970), which appeared after I had completed this study, offers the most detailed and interesting complement to my approach. Stressing the use of the grotesque and the reduction of human life to surfaces, Hendin argues that Flannery O'Connor was temperamentally of the devil's party, an argument first made by John Hawkes.

Chapter 1

1. "Remarks on the Southern Religion," *I'll Take My Stand*, by Twelve Southerners (New York: Harper & Brothers, 1930), p. 157.
2. *Science and Wisdom*, trans. Bernard Wall (New York: Charles Scribner's Sons, 1940), p. 84.
3. Flannery O'Connor, *Mystery and Manners*, ed. Sally and Robert Fitzgerald (New York: Farrar, Straus & Giroux, 1969), p. 156.
4. See *Integral Humanism: Temporal and Spiritual Problems of a New Christendom*, trans. Joseph W. Evans (New York: Charles Scribner's Sons, 1968). The original French edition was published in 1936.
5. *Freedom, Grace, and Destiny*, trans. John Murray (London: Harvill Press, 1961), p. 9.
6. *The Nature and Destiny of Man* (New York: Charles Scribner's Sons, 1943), 1, 288–89.
7. *Theology of Culture*, ed. Robert C. Kimball (New York: Oxford University Press, 1959), p. 210.

Notes

8. "Flannery O'Connor and the Grotesque," *The Added Dimension: The Mind and Art of Flannery O'Connor*, ed. Melvin J. Friedman and Lewis A. Lawson (New York: Fordham University Press, 1966), pp. 108–22. John Hawkes, who was more interested in Miss O'Connor's literary technique than in the ways in which she preserved her sanity in a mad world, was more tentative in interpreting her authorial points of view. He admitted that the "devil" he found in her writing might be "only a metaphor, a way of referring to a temperament strong enough and sympathetic enough to sustain the work of piercing pretention" ("Flannery O'Connor's Devil," *Sewanee Review*, 70 [1962], 406).

9. *A Good Man Is Hard to Find* (New York: Harcourt, Brace and Company, 1955), p. 88. This edition, hereafter abbreviated as *Good Man*, is used throughout this study. Page notations hereinafter will be given in the text.

10. *The Faith and Modern Man*, trans. Charlotte E. Forsyth (New York: Pantheon Books, 1952), p. 109.

11. Compare, for example, Romano Guardini's discussion of spiritual crises and the awakening of sexuality (ibid., pp. 102–103).

12. *The Sickness Unto Death*, trans. Walter Lowrie (Princeton: Princeton University Press, 1941), p. 17.

13. *The Nature and Destiny of Man*, 1, 55.

14. *Systematic Theology* (Chicago: University of Chicago Press, 1951–63), 2, 42–43.

15. *The Sane Society* (New York: Rinehart & Company, 1955), p. 120.

16. "Everyman as Pervert," *Angel in Armor: A Post-Freudian Perspective on the Nature of Man* (New York: George Braziller, 1969), pp. 3–38.

17. *The Phenomenon of Man*, trans. Bernard Wall (New York: Harper & Row, 1959), p. 267.

Chapter 2

1. Denis de Rougemont, *Love in the Western World*, trans. Montgomery Belgion, rev. ed. (New York: Pantheon Books, 1956); M. C. D'Arcy, *The Mind and Heart of Love* (London: Faber and Faber, 1945).

2. Paul Tillich, *The Shaking of the Foundations* (New York: Charles Scribner's Sons, 1948), p. 128; *Theology of Culture*, p. 27.

3. *The Sickness Unto Death*, p. 23.

4. *The Concept of Dread*, trans. Walter Lowrie (Princeton: Princeton University Press, 1957), pp. 86–92.

5. *Freedom, Grace, and Destiny*, p. 207.

6. Remembering Miss O'Connor's interest in Nathanael West's novels, one might recall his similar accounts of people who are fascinated with cemeteries, funerals, and disasters.

7. Coincidentally, Swiss playwright Max Frisch worked similarly with this problem in *Biedermann and the Firebugs*, which he wrote as a radio

play in 1953 but which was not staged until 1958. (Miss O'Connor's story first appeared in the spring of 1954.) Although the play has strong political implications for people under incipient totalitarianism, it generally explores the timidity, impotence, and defensive optimism of a bourgeois Everyman who believes that, if he is polite and trusting, the psychopathic firebugs in his attic will not burn down his house. The main themes of both the play and Miss O'Connor's story resemble Maritain's claim that the man of bourgeois liberalism has tried to deny man's irrationality, with disastrous consequences for his psyche and his society (*Integral Humanism*, p. 79).

8. *The Sickness Unto Death*, pp. 64–65.

9. Thomas M. Lorch, "Flannery O'Connor: A Christian Allegorist," *Critique*, 10 (1968), 76–77. He also finds this fault in "The Enduring Chill" and "The Artificial Nigger," both of which will be discussed in terms of this problem later in this study.

10. *Everything That Rises Must Converge* (New York: Farrar, Straus & Giroux, 1965), pp. 195–96. This edition, hereafter abbreviated as *Everything*, is used throughout this study with page notations given in the text.

11. "Writing for the Theatre," *The New British Drama*, ed. Henry Popkin (New York: Grove Press, 1964), p. 580.

12. The references to Kierkegaard in the next few pages refer to *The Sickness Unto Death*, pp. 107–19. The sexual categories of despair are clearly metaphorical. For Kierkegaard, and in Flannery O'Connor's works, men or women may be in either kind of despair.

13. Perhaps The Misfit did not actually kill his father. The psychiatrist could have meant that his patient had symbolically killed the father through rebellious crimes, and The Misfit could have taken that explanation literally, thinking that he was falsely accused of parricide. This reading also would reveal the Oedipal and religious themes that I discuss, but it would require minor changes in the symbolism because the repressed and sublimated desire to kill the father would replace the actual killing. The rest of the pattern would remain the same, for The Misfit's amnesia would be as appropriate to symbolic, as it would be to literal, parricide and the symbolic acts of defiance would have as much psychological and religious significance as the archetypal impulses they represent.

14. This description strongly anticipates Dostoevski's underground man, with whom The Misfit has much in common, as he does with Dostoevski's active despairers, Raskolnikov and Ivan Karamazov. This is not to say that Miss O'Connor was directly influenced by Dostoevski, any more than she was by Kierkegaard. Most likely the similarities in all three are caused mainly by similar combinations of Christian faith and perceptive concern with the psychology of disbelief.

15. Carter W. Martin, *The True Country: Themes in the Fiction of Flannery O'Connor* (Nashville: Vanderbilt University Press, 1969), p. 148.

16. *The Mind and Heart of Love*, chap. 9 (esp. pp. 210–11).

17. *The Concept of Dread*, p. 125.

18. Joel Wells, "Off the Cuff," *Critic*, quoted in *The Added Dimension*, p. 255.

Chapter 3

1. *Systematic Theology*, 2, 54.
2. Lorch, p. 77.
3. Martin, pp. 39–40.
4. "An American Girl," p. 128.
5. See, for example, Wylie Sypher, "The Meanings of Comedy," *Comedy* (Garden City, New York: Doubleday & Company, 1956) and Northrop Frye, "The Mythos of Spring: Comedy," *Anatomy of Criticism* (Princeton: Princeton University Press, 1957).
6. "An American Girl," p. 128.
7. *The Sickness Unto Death*, p. 54.
8. *The Shaking of the Foundations*, p. 90.

Chapter 4

1. *Wise Blood*, 2nd ed., with Author's Note (New York: Farrar, Straus & Cudahy, 1962), p. 22. This edition is cited throughout this study, with page notations given in the text.
2. *Fear and Trembling*, trans. Walter Lowrie (Princeton: Princeton University Press, 1945), pp. 102–23. Miss O'Connor's statement in 1963 that "our response to life is different if we have been taught only a definition of faith than if we have trembled with Abraham as he held the knife over Isaac" (*Mystery and Manners*, pp. 202–203) suggests a conception of faith quite similar to Kierkegaard's and, more tenuously, to Pascal's.
3. See *Beyond the Pleasure Principle* and *Civilization and Its Discontents*; also Theodor Reik, *Masochism in Modern Man*, trans. Margaret H. Beigel and Gertrude M. Kurth (New York: Farrar, Strauss, 1949); Norman O. Brown, *Life Against Death* (Middletown, Conn.: Wesleyan University Press, 1959); Herbert Marcuse, *Eros and Civilization* (Boston: The Beacon Press, 1955).
4. Introduction to *Everything That Rises Must Converge*, pp. xv–xvi.
5. An interview with Granville Hicks, "A Writer at Home with Her Heritage," *Saturday Review*, 45 (May 12, 1962), 22; quoted in *The Added Dimension*, p. 258.
6. Malin, "O'Connor and the Grotesque"; Louis Rubin, "Flannery O'Connor and the Bible Belt," *The Added Dimension*, pp. 49–72.
7. *The Violent Bear It Away* (New York: Farrar, Straus & Cudahy, 1960), p. 5. This edition is used throughout this study.
8. The distinctiveness and possibilities of the subplot are shown by its later transformation into the novella "The Lame Shall Enter First." There, Tarwater is flattened into Rufus Johnson, a symbolic foil for Sheppard, the City Recreational Director into which Rayber has been transformed. In the

novella Miss O'Connor resumed the more familiar pattern of her stories. Sheppard does not feel the emotional conflicts that Rayber does, nor is he as conscious of his struggles and their causes. Instead, he is one of the dedicatedly self-satified characters who is made suddenly to confront his own guilt. By contrasting Rayber and Sheppard, both in character and development, one can see clearly how Miss O'Connor had used Rayber to parallel the Tarwaters in her novel.

9. According to Fitzgerald, p. xxv.

10. "O'Connor and the Bible Belt."

Index

Index

David Eggenschwiler is associate professor of English at the University of Southern California. He received his B.A. degree (1958) in psychology from Harvard University, his M.A. (1961) in English from Arizona State University, and his Ph.D. (1965) in English from Stanford University.

The manuscript was edited by Linda Grant. The book and jacket were designed by Joanne Kinney. The typeface for the text is Linotype Electra designed by W. A. Dwiggins about 1935 for Mergenthaler, and the display face is Weiss designed by Emil Rudolf Weiss in 1931.

The text is printed on Oxford Paper Company's Book Text paper and the book is bound in Columbia Mills' Fictionette Natural Finish cloth over binders' boards. Manufactured in the United States of America.